VEDIC RELIGION
AND
PHILOSOPHY

BY
SWAMI PRABHAVANANDA, 1893-
(Head of the Vedanta Centre, Hollywood, U. S. A.)

Written under the Editorial Supervision of
DR. P. H. HOUSTON
*(Professor of English, Occidental College, Los Angeles,
California, U.S.A.)*

SRI RAMAKRISHNA MATH
MYLAPORE, MADRAS (INDIA)

Published by
THE PRESIDENT
SRI RAMAKRISHNA MATH
MYLAPORE, MADRAS

Copyright by
SWAMI PRABHAVANANDA

FOURTH IMPRESSION
xxii-9-57

THE JUPITER PRESS PRIVATE LTD., MADRAS-18.

PREFACE

The purpose of *Vedic Religion and Philosophy* is not primarily to add to the vast literature of scholarly interpretation of Indian philosophy and religion, though it is the fervent hope of the author that it will meet the severest scholarly tests. It is rather to make as wide an appeal as possible to the growing body of intelligent interest in Indian philosophy and civilization.

Our thanks are due to Mr. V. Subramanya Iyer, President, Board of Sanskrit Studies and Examination, Mysore, and Reader in Philosophy to His Highness the Maharaja of Mysore, for his valuable suggestions and criticisms.

Vivekananda Home   PRABHAVANANDA
Hollywood, California, U.S.A.

CONTENTS

CHAPTER I

THE SPIRIT OF INDIAN PHILOSOPHY

THE word *Darshana*, which is usually translated
The Relation between Religion and Philosophy. as 'philosophy', means in Sanskrit 'seeing' or 'experience'.
From this we may gather that
Indian philosophy or religion is not merely metaphysical speculation, but has its foundation in the
immediate data of experience. The verities of life
like God and soul are regarded by the Hindu mind,
not as concepts speculative and problematical, as
is the case in Western philosophy, but as definitely
experienced truths. These ultimate truths can be
experienced not merely by a chosen few, but under
right conditions, by all humanity.

This insistence upon direct experience rather than
on abstract reasoning is what distinguishes Indian
philosophy of religion from philosophy as Western
nations know it. This direct experience is the
source from which all Indian thought flows, and it
is the accepted basis of philosophy in India.

This experience, it must be made clear, is not
of the senses, nor must it be confused with the
operations of the intellect, nor with emotional
experience ; it is super-sensuous and transcendental,
not to be completely explained in rational terms.

The *Mandukya Upanishad* speaks of three states of consciousness—waking, dreaming, and dreamless sleep. These three states are common to all. In addition to these there is the Fourth, or the *Turiya* —the transcendental state which may be described as the innate nature of consciousness. Though it is present in all, man does not recognise it in his ignorant state. Indian philosophers call this trans-cendental state by various names, but all of them unmistakably point to the same goal.

From the foregoing we may comprehend the relation between Indian religion and Indian phi-losophy. Religion to a Hindu is not, however, the common Western conception of faith, nor does it merely comprise dogmas and creeds. It is rather *Anubhuti* — realization and experience. Swami Brahmananda, my spiritual master and a great saint of modern India, once told me, "Spiritual life begins after one enters into *Samadhi* (the trans-cendental state)." Religion is therefore not divorced from philosophy ; the latter, in fact, is an attempt to present ultimate truths, already realized in experience, in terms of the rationalising intellect.

Professor Max Muller has declared that philosophy was recommended in India 'not for the sake of knowledge, but for the highest purpose that man can strive after in this life'. In India, philosophers are saints, and saints are philosophers.

This fact of *Samadhi* or the transcendental state of consciousness is a matter of experience throughout the whole history of Indian life. Today, as well as in earliest times, it has been experienced. Sri Ramakrishna, the greatest saint of modern India, though not a learned man, attained *Samadhi,* and, having realized the highest illumination, spoke words of solace and wisdom to all men. So also this state is attainable by any one who strives to purify himself from the dross of worldliness.

The Hindu mind, however, is careful not to **The Place of** confuse reveries, dreams, hallucina-**Reason.** tions and hypnotic spells with transcendental experience. So certain proofs of its validity and its relation both to life in general, and to reason in particular, are taken into consideration.

The first condition or test of this transcendental truth must be, in the words of Jaimini (founder of the *Purva Mimamsa* school of thought), ' *Arthe Anupalabdhe* '—that is, the revelation should be related to ' something which is otherwise unknown and unknowable '. The transcendental revelation is therefore not a revelation of things or truths normally perceived or generally known, nor of truths capable of perception and of being known through the ordinary instruments of knowledge. And yet this transcendental truth must be universally understandable in relation to human experience, and must be communicable to us in terms of known experience.

The next condition or test of truth is that the revealed truth must not contradict other *Pramanas* or proofs. It is necessarily beyond and above reason, but it must not contradict reason.

Thus Indian philosophy, though having its foundations in personal revelation, gives a legitimate place to logic and reason, and there has never been any check to the growth of philosophic thinking. In fact, no other race has produced a succession of more subtle or more rigidly logical thinkers than the Hindus ; only, without exception, they have declared that reason, unaided by transcendental experience, is blind. Those who are called orthodox philosophers, as we shall see, accept the *Vedic* scriptures as recording revealed truths ; and they make these scriptures the basis of their reasoning. Sankara, one of the foremost philosophers of India, has this to say concerning the part reason plays in the investigation of truth : " As the thoughts of man are altogether unfettered, reasoning, which disregards the holy texts and rests on individual opinion, has no proper foundation. We see how arguments, which some clever men had excogitated with great pains, are shown by people still more ingenious, to be fallacious, and how the arguments of the latter again are refuted in their turn by other men ; so that, on account of the diversity of men's opinions, it is impossible to accept mere reasoning as having a sure foundation." [1]

[1] Sankara, while explaining the final cause and substance of the universe, further remarks as follows : " Perfect knowledge has the characteristic mark of uniformity because it depends on accomplished, actually existing

The systems of Indian philosophy fall into two

The Authority of the Vedas. main divisions, according as they do or do not accept the authority of the *Vedas*. That is to say, all systems except Buddhism and Jainism are pronounced *Astika* or orthodox ; the two latter, which deny the authority of the great primary scriptures, are *Nastika* or heterodox. If, however, we accept the literal meaning of the word *Astika* as belief in existence after death, then all systems of thought, with the exception of the materialism of Charvaka, are *Astika*.

things : for whatever thing is permanently of one and the same nature is acknowledged to be a true or real thing, and knowledge conversant about such is called perfect knowledge ; as, for instance, the knowledge embodied in the proposition, ' Fire is hot '. Sow it is clear that in the case of perfect knowledge a mutual conflict of men's opinions is impossible. But that cognitions founded on reasoning do conflict is generally known ; for we continually observe that what one logician endeavours to establish as perfect knowledge is demolished by another, who, in his turn, is treated alike by a third. How, therefore, can knowledge, which is founded on reasoning, and whose object is not something permanently uniform, be perfect knowledge ? Nor can we collect at a given moment and on a given spot all the logicians of the past, present, and future time, so as to settle that their opinion regarding some uniform object is to be considered perfect knowledge. The *Veda,* on the other hand, which is eternal and the source of knowledge, may be allowed to have for its object firmly established things, and hence the perfection of that knowledge which is founded on the *Veda* cannot be denied by any of the logicians of the past, present, or future. We have thus established the perfection of this, our knowledge, which reposes on the *Upanishad,* and, as apart from it, perfect knowledge is impossible. Our final position, therefore, is that on the ground of scripture and of reasoning, subordinate to scripture, the intelligent *Brahman* is to be considered the cause and substance of the world." (From the translation of Sankara's commentary on the *Vedanta Sutras,* by G. Thibaut.)

What Charvaka really taught, or whether there was a philosopher named Charvaka at all, it is difficult to know, for we hear of him only through the refutation of his philosophy of sensualism by various other schools of thought. It is, in effect, but the simple philosophy of scepticism which runs as a cross-current in every age and every country. The name Charvaka literally means ' sweet word '.

Some Oriental scholars translate this word Nastika as atheist. But if this meaning of the word is applied to Buddhism and Jainism because they reject an anthropomorphic God, then many of the orthodox schools are similarly at fault. The *Sankhya* philosophy, for example, denies God as creator, yet it is held to be orthodox.

Curiously, there is no equivalent in Sanskrit for the word ' atheism '. In the *Gita* mention is made of those who do not believe in God, the Intelligent Principle, and these are said to be of ' deluded intellect '.

We have declared that the *Vedas* or *Sruti* (the revealed truths) stand as an absolute authority behind which the orthodox schools cannot go. In this sense their authority might seem to resemble apparently the position held by the Holy Bible in many periods of Christian thought ; but in the words of Dr. S. Radhakrishnan, " This appeal to the *Vedas* does not involve any reference to any extra-philo-sophical standard. What is dogma to the ordinary man is experience to the pure in heart." With the exception of Buddhism and Jainism, all schools of thought regard the *Vedas* as recording the transcendental experience of the first mighty seers of ancient India. These experiences, because they have become standard for all Hindus, cannot and should not contradict those in any other age. Furthermore they are the truths experienced and experienceable in every age and every country by all who are pure in heart. For this reason, all Hindus believe that the Vedas are eternal, beginningless and without end. Transcendental experience therefore has received its standard expression in these Indo-Aryan scriptures.

It is true that, though all orthodox Indian philosophers regard the *Vedas* as eternal—without beginning or end—some limit these eternal laws to the records in the *Vedas,* the Indo-Aryan scriptures. Transcendental experiences of other ages and other countries, though not denied their due authority, are regarded by them not as *Vedas* or *Sruti,* but as *Agamas.* A distinction is thus drawn between the *Vedas* and the *Agamas*, though the *Vedas* are still regarded as beginningless and endless. In the words of the learned Professor M. Hiriyanna, "We may deduce a distinction between the two from a fourth condition sometimes laid down (*cf. Kusumanjali,* II, 3), that the revealed truth should have proved acceptable to the general mind of the community (*Mahajana-parigraha*), or that it should be in harmony with what may be described as race-intuition.

It is this sanction of the community in general that in the end seems to distinguish orthodox *Sruti* from heterodox *Agama*."

This distinction is arbitrary and seems opposed to the very definition and spirit of the *Vedas*. Whatever a particular community may or may not sanction, a revealed truth is a direct experience, and as such it must be in the same category of revealed truth as the *Vedas*. But at the same time, we must naturally exert great care in judging the validity of any particular revelation, so that it does not contradict the experiences of other seers and the recorded standard experiences that we may read in the Indo-Aryan *Vedas*.

What then of Buddhism and Jainism? Shall we discard them from among the highest expressions of Indian thought? They do in fact accept the authority of revealed knowledge and transcendental experience, though they deny the authority of the *Vedas*, particularly of the ritualistic portions, as a result of certain particular historical circumstances. They were born at a time when the spirit of the *Vedas* had been lost, and the Hindus held faithfully to the letter of the law, and priestcraft reigned supreme. Religion then confined itself to sacrificial rites. The yearning to know the truth of the self or *Brahman* in one's own soul, which is attained only by the pure in heart, was wanting. Buddha, though he denied the authority of the *Vedas*, actually impressed their real spirit upon his

followers by urging them to live the life of pure
conduct in order to free themselves from the burden
of sorrow. And he showed the way by himself
attaining *Nirvana* or the transcendental state of
consciousness.

Thus the teachings of Buddha as well as those of
Mahavira, founder of Jainism, do not contradict
the spirit of the *Vedas* but are in entire harmony
with it.

From the foregoing it can be readily seen that
The Central Pro- Indian philosophy of religion is
blem of Indian fundamentally mystic and spirit-
Philosophy. ual. "Indian philosophy," says
Professor M. Hiriyanna, "aims beyond logic. This
peculiarity is to be ascribed to the fact that
philosophy in India did not take its rise in wonder
or curiosity as it seems to have done in the West ;
rather under the pressure of a practical need
arising from the presence of physical evil in life.
It is the problem of how to remove this evil that
troubled the ancient Indians most, and *Moksha*
in all the systems represents a state in which it
is, in one sense or another, taken to have been overcome. Philosophic endeavour was directed primarily
to find a remedy for the ills of life, and the consideration of metaphysical questions came in as a matter
of course."

This, then, is the central problem of Indian
philosophy—an overmastering sense of the evil of
physical existence, combined with a search for

release from pain and sorrow—and in this respect, it is distinguished from the philosophies of any other race or country.

We are led here to a consideration of the charge of pessimism brought against Indian philosophy by the West—the charge that it springs, as Chailley declares, 'from lassitude and a desire for rest'. This criticism by those who, as in the West, seek fulfilment through positive aggressive action, arises from a misunderstanding of the purpose of Indian philosophy. This philosophy is *pessimistic,* if by that word is meant the acknowledgement of the nature of life in this world,—that it is a strange mingling of good and evil, that life on the plane of the senses yields but a doubtful happiness, and that physical and moral evils continue to the end of our mortal existence. The distinctive characteristic of Indian philosophy lies in the fact that it is not merely dissatisfied with existing suffering, but that it points out the path towards the attainment of *Moksha* or release, which is a state of unalloyed and infinite bliss, and of freedom from all earthly suffering.

Philosophers differ, however, with respect to the exact nature of this goal of *Moksha,* and of the methods to be employed in attaining it; and these differences make up the substance of Hindu thought. They are due to the varying grades of experience in realizing transcendental life rather than to a great diversity of opinion with respect to it.

And of course it is above all due to the attempt
to express the inexpressible.

In one thing, however, they all agree. That is
that spiritual perfection can be attained in this life.
"Man's aim," says Professor Hiriyanna, "was no
longer represented as the attainment of perfection in
a hypothetical hereafter, but a continual progress
towards it within the limits of the present life."
Moksha, or the attainment of freedom from the
limitations and sufferings of physical life, is the
supreme aspiration of Indian philosophy.[1]

Sankara, speaking of the supreme goal of human
life, says, "A man is born not to desire life in
the world of the senses, but to realize the bliss of
Jivanmukti." And the *Upanishads* over and again
emphasize this truth, "Blessed is he who attains
illumination in this very life ; otherwise it is his
greatest calamity." But it is immediately pointed
out that if a man fails to attain the supreme goal
in this life, he must attain it in some other life, for
he will be given many opportunities by rebirths to
reach the goal of perfection.

[1] The *Purva Mimamsa,* one of the six philosophical
systems of India, is an apparent exception to what we have
just said ; for it does not speak of *Moksha* or release, but
rather teaches work and sacrifices for heaven and the
enjoyments thereof. But, though this philosophy does not
include *Moksha* as the direct goal of its striving, indirectly
it does. For work, as taught by Jaimini, brings purification of the heart, which leads one to *Moksha.*. If, however,
we take *Purva* and *Uttara Mimamsa* as forming one system
of thought, then we may declare that, without exception, Indian philosophies set forth *Moksha* as the ultimate
goal which may be attained in this life.

This failure to attain direct experience of the truth, and consequently of freedom, is due to man's ignorance, which is universal, and which forms the chief cause of sin and suffering. It can be dispelled by direct knowledge of ultimate truth through purification of the heart, and a constant striving for detachment of the soul from worldly desires. By transcending the limitations of the body, the mind and the senses, one may enter the superconscious state of experience.

The methods of attaining this higher state of consciousness are hearing, reasoning, and meditating upon the ultimate reality. One must first hear of it from the *Sruti* or the *Vedas*. Then one must reason upon it. Finally comes meditation upon it in order to realize the truth for oneself. Different schools offer different methods of attaining the same goal, and the practice of *Yoga*, or the exercises prescribed in the art of concentration and meditation, constitutes a salient part of Indian religious life.

To tread the path of philosophy is to seek after truth and follow a way of life. Before a man sets out on this quest after truth, he must fulfil certain conditions. Sankara sums them up as follows : First, there must be discrimination between the real and the unreal. This statement means, not that he must possess a complete knowledge of absolute reality, which is attained only as a culmination of long practice, but that he must unfailingly subject the nature of things to a rigid analysis by discriminating between what is transitory and what is abiding, or between what is true and what is false.

The second condition is detachment from the selfiish enjoyments of this or a future life. The aspirant must learn that the highest good is realized not through material pleasure, but through a continuous search for the Infinite, the Abiding Joy. This ideal of renunciation must be realized by a gradual purification of the seeker's heart and soul. So a third condition is prescribed whereby the student may acquire tranquillity of the mind, self-control, patience, poice, burning faith in the ideal, and self-surrender. These are called the six treasures of life. The thirst for *Moksha* or liberation is the fourth condition. "The people of India," says Dr. S. Radhakrishnan, "have such an immense respect for these philosophers who glory in the might of knowledge and the power of intellect, that they worship them. The prophetic souls who, with a noble passion for truth, strive hard to understand the mystery of the world and give utterance to it, spending laborious days and sleepless nights, are philosophers in a vital sense of the term."

Deliverance from ignorance and entrance upon the path of illumination come only through annihilation of the false ego. "When the ego dies, all troubles cease," says Sri Ramakrishna. Such a condition of being does not, however, imply the loss of one's individuality, but rather the attainment of a greater individuality, for we can lose nothing

that is real. Kalidasa, the great Hindu poet and
dramatist, has beautifully expressed the idea when
he says that the ideal of renunciation consists
in owning the whole world while disowning one's
own self.

What then is the relation of psychology and ethics
Place of Psycho- to Indian religious philosophy?
logy and Ethics. The science of psychology, as
Westerners know it, is man's attempt to explain the
behaviour and the operations of his mind with reference to his body and the stimuli received through his
senses. Ethics is the formulation of the science of
conduct in relation to society as man faces his multi-
farious activities as a social being. Do these
two interpretations of man's material life enter into
the consideration of the philosophies of India?

They do, in a very definite way. As a matter of
fact, Indian philosophy and Indian psychology are
not merely allied subjects, but the latter is actually
an integral part of the former. To the Hindu mind,
psychology has its inception in the thinking self and
not in the objects of thought. It is not content
with merely stating the working of the mind in the
normal planes of consciousness as is the case with
our modern system of behaviourism, but it points
out how the mind ranges beyond the ordinary
conscious plane of psychic activity, and how the
resulting experiences are even more real than
the experiences of the objective world. It also
differs from the psycho-analysis of Freud in that,

though it accepts the sub-conscious mind, it claims that man is capable of controlling his sub-conscious impressions as well as his conscious mind, and of attaining to the superconscious state, which no school of Western psychology has yet taken into consideration. By teaching the normal mind methods of restraining its own vagaries, with the aim of gaining supreme mastery over itself, and of ultimately rising above it, Indian philosophy distinguishes itself from all other known systems of philosophy or psychology. The *Yoga* system of Patanjali deals specifically with this process of mind control.

The problem of ethics is also a problem of Indian philosophy. Though not actually identified with Hindu philosophy, ethics is its very foundation. Philosophy seeks to transcend the mere life of conduct so that ethics remains the means for its own supererogation. Moreover, Hindu ethics concerns itself not only with outer human activity, but extends to inner life as well. Every teaching is conditioned by the phrase, ' in thought, word, and deed '. Ways and methods of conduct are explicitly revealed, which, if followed, will enable one naturally to live the ethical life. The emphasis is laid upon the ultimate transformation of the whole being when one rises above the injunctions of moral codes. He is not troubled, we read in the *Upanishads,* by thoughts like these : Have I not done the right ? Have I done the wrong ? Bhavabhuti, a Sanskrit poet says, appropriately : " An ordinary man is truthful when the words follow the fact. But the saint's words are followed by facts." Such is the relation between saintliness and truthfulness.

Indian philosophy is thus not a mere way of thinking but a way of life, a way of light, and a way of truth. To become a philosopher is to become transformed in life, renewed in mind, and baptized in spirit.

CHAPTER II

THE VEDAS AND THEIR TEACHINGS

I

Peace Chant. MAY my speech be united with the mind, and may my mind be united with the speech.

O Thou Self-luminous (*Brahman*), may Thy light shine forth in me (by removing the veil of ignorance).

Do Thou reveal the spirit of the *Vedas* unto me.

May the truth of the *Vedas* never forsake me.

May I seek day and night (to realize) what I learn from my study. May I speak the truth (*Brahman*).

May I speak the truth.

May It (*Brahman*) protect me.

May It protect my teacher.

Om Peace, Peace, Peace.

—*The Rig Veda*

II

Origin of the Vedas. With the important exceptions of Buddhism and Jainism, all schools of Indian philosophy and all sects of Indian religion recognize in the *Vedas* their origin and final authority. This is true even of all those

2

sects and schools which have arisen in modern times. What is known as Hinduism or Hindu philosophy is in reality a misnomer ; it should be properly called the *Vedic* religion, which is also the universally accepted religion and philosophy of modern India known as *Vedanta*.

Even more than the other scriptures of the world, the *Vedas* make a special claim to be Divine in their origin. Whereas the *Bible,* the *Koran,* and other revelations of the Word of God owe their sacred authority either to Divine inspiration, or to delivery of the sacred message through an angel or other special messenger from God unto certain chosen persons, the *Vedas* are said to be *Apaurusheya* or simply Divine in their origin. They are themselves authority, being the knowledge of God.

This mysterious distinction between the Indo-Aryan scriptures and other Divine revelations needs some elucidation.

Yo vedebhyah akhilam jagat nirmame.—" God created the whole universe out of the knowledge of the *Vedas*." (That is to say, *Vedic* knowledge comes even before creation.) In these words of Sayana-charya, the learned commentator on the *Vedas,* is expressed the universal belief regarding them. So the attempt to discover the date of the origin of the *Vedas* is like trying to discover the origin of the knowledge of God, or of God Himself. The search for the beginning of the *Vedic* literature is similar to the search for the origin of the universe. While it is true that the universe has undergone an evolution from primitive forms through successive stages to its present stage of development, the *Vedas* are themselves a completed development.

Indian philosophers are of course believers in the theory of evolution. They were in fact evolutionists long before the word evolution meant anything to the Western world. But they insisted that evolution implies involution, which means that the present universe is only one of a series of universes existing from the past, and that there can therefore be no beginning to creation. So to the Indian mind creation is without beginning and without end. Every *Brahmin* boy repeats daily this *Vedic* prayer, " The sun and the moon the Lord created like the suns and the moons of previous cycles."

What a Hindu means when he declares that the *Vedas* are eternal is not that the particular books which contain the scriptures have lasted from the beginning of time. Just as creation is infinite and eternal, without beginning and without end, so is the Knowledge of God ; and this knowledge is what is meant by the *Vedas*. At the beginning of a cycle, this knowledge is made manifest, to return, when the cycle ends, to its unmanifested state. It is mere sophistry to claim that these books, the Indo-Aryan scriptures, are eternal ; what really deserve to be called eternal are the great laws of God discovered and recorded in these books by the *Rishis,* the seers of thought who have lived close to God in every

age. They discovered these spiritual laws by
directly perceiving them while in a transcendental
state of consciousness. And these truths can be
perceived again and again at all times and in all ages
through this same means. In the words of Swami
Vivekananda, "Of all the scriptures of the world, it
is the *Vedas* alone that declare that even the study
of the *Vedas* is secondary. The real study is that
' by which we realize the unchangeable '." (*cf.*
Mundaka Upanishad.)

In the *Purusha Sukta* of the *Rig Veda* we read
thus about the origin of the *Vedas* : "The gods
then performed a sacrificial rite mentally, meditating
on the transcendental *Purusha* as the sacrifice itself.
From that sacrifice, which is the *Purusha* (the
Transcendental Being), came out *Rik, Sama,* and
Yajus (the different *Vedas*)."

Another passage in the *Satapatha Brahmana* of
the *Vedas* reads, "As clouds of smoke come out
from a damp wood on fire, so have the *Vedas* come
out like breath from the Supreme Being." According to tradition, *Brahma* (the creator in the Hindu
trinity) first received the knowledge contained in
the *Vedas,* and from *Brahma* it descended to the
Rishis, who are born in the beginning of each cycle.
At the beginning of a cycle are born *Rishis* with
perfect knowledge, which they come to be endowed
with by virtue of the high stage of evolution reached
by them in previous cycles ; they are therefore the
special messengers of God for the transmission of

knowledge of Him through the great cycles of creation.

So it is the belief of all Hindus that in the very earliest stage of each cycle of creation, there are born on earth highly evolved souls as well as primitive people, and that it is through these former types that religion first enters the world. This belief in full intellectual and spiritual maturity, without the necessity of a social process of gradual unfoldment, distinguishes the Hindu theory of the origin of religion from that held by Western scholars, namely, that religion has evolved from primitive forms of Nature worship and fetish ritual. The Hindu theory of evolution is one of a continuous birth of worlds in an infinite series, with the knowledge of God descending throughout the entire process.

We may readily understand, therefore, how impossible it is to fix any date for the origin of *Vedic* knowledge. The extant records as revealed in the Indo-Aryan scriptures are accepted as of Divine origin, and they may be called, without fear of contradiction, the earliest spiritual records in the world. They are not primitive in their ideas and conceptions of spiritual life ; on the contrary they contain the truly lofty metaphysical and spiritual ideas that have inspired saints and philosophers from earliest times, and continue to be the source of spiritual life in India even today.

It is true that we can discover in the *Vedas* ideas apparently primitive by the side of these others that are indicative of the highest spiritual inspiration. That is because these scriptures represent the intellectual gropings of primitive men as well as the conceptions of the Deity and spiritual life held by men of the highest intellectual and spiritual advancement. There are present in these books both higher and lower forms of thought ; for, just as today, religious teaching always conforms to the capacity of those who would receive it. The *Vedas* reveal both genuine inspiration on the part of a few divinely gifted men and women, and a slow fumbling search for spiritual consolation on the part of a great many others.

III

Traditional Indian legends give the following account of the beginning of *Vedic* literature :

Legendary Account of the Origin of the Vedas.

Once upon a time, before the historic account of man was attempted, *Brahma*, the first-born of God, was meditating upon the Supreme *Brahman* when, through His grace, there was manifested within the shrine of his heart the eternal Word Om (the Logos), the seed of all knowledge and of all thought.[1] There were also manifest one by one all the sounds of the different letters. Through these letters there became known unto *Brahma,* the knowledge of the

[1] *Cf.* The Platonic philosophy of Logos—the identity of word and thought. See also the Gospel according to St. John—" In the beginning was the Word, and the Word was with God, and the Word was God."

Vedas. In order to spread this knowledge throughout the world, he taught it to his disciples like
Marichi, Atri, Angiras, and other *Rishis.* In this
way the *Vedas* became known to all humanity.

After many cycles came *Dvapara Yuga* (perhaps
the Copper Age). The Lord Narayana incarnated
Himself as the son of the *Rishi* Parasara and
Mother Satyavati, taking the name Krishna-
Dvaipayana. To give the *Vedas* greater simplicity,
he compiled and divided them into four parts, namely, the *Rik,* the *Sama,* the *Yajus,* and the *Atharva,*
and taught each of them to his four chief disciples,
Paila, Vaisampayana, Jaimini, and Sumantu, who
in turn taught the *Vedas* to their disciples.[1]

An interesting legend is told about *Yajur Veda*
and its teacher, Vaisampayana, who had under him
several disciples. On a certain occasion many *Rishis*
met together for a conference at which it was
desired that all *Rishis* should be present. " Whoever
fails to attend," they announced, " will commit
a great sin, equal to that of killing a *Brahmin.*"
Now the great *Rishi* Vaisampayana failed to attend,
and as a consequence, the curse of all the *Rishis*
fell upon him. In order to expiate the sin he
requested his disciples to practise austerities. One
disciple, Yajnavalkya by name, however, said,
" Master, how can you expiate your sin by the

---

[1] In India there still live *Brahmins* claiming to be des-
cendants of these *Vedic* seers. And they are followers of
one or another of the *Vedas.*

austerities of these thy worthless disciples? I am the one amongst them who can bring good unto thee by my practices." At this the master grew angry and said, "How dare you speak so? I do not like to have such a hot-headed egotistical disciple as you. Give back what you have learned from me and be off."

So the egotist Yajnavalkya cast from him what he had learned and went forth. The other *Rishis,* not enduring this insult to their knowledge, assumed the forms of *Tittiri* birds and gathered up the knowledge that had just been ejected, and taught it to their own disciples. And this knowledge was thenceforth known as *Krishna-Yajur Veda,* and the branch, as *Taittiriya.*

Now Yajnavalkya, having cast out knowledge of the *Vedas,* felt how empty he was, as he realized what a very beast a man becomes without any *Vedic* knowledge. Where then might he find a teacher? And it came to him that the sun god is never separated from the *Vedas*; for in the morning he is adorned with the *Rig Veda,* at noon with the *Yajur Veda,* and in the evening with the *Sama Veda.* And so, accepting the sun god as his teacher, Yajnavalkya prayed to him for knowledge. The sun god, pleased with the devotion of his new votary, taught him the *Vedas.* This particular branch of knowledge was thenceforth known as *Sukla-Yajur Veda.* Yajnavalkya then taught it to his disciples.

According to tradition, none can study the *Vedas* without a teacher. " Approach a teacher," it is said in the *Vedas*, " being ' *Samitpani* ', with humility and a spirit of service." Only thus can the spirit of the *Vedas* be revealed.

The following hymn from the *Satapatha Brahmana* describes the good effects of such study :

" The study and teaching of the *Vedas* are pleasing
    indeed.
He who follows this attains concentrated mind,
He does not become a slave to his passions ;
His desires come true, and he rests happily.
Verily does he become a healer of his own self,
Self-controlled,   devoted,   with   well-cultivated
    mind.
He attains fame and does good to the world."

IV

Indian philosophers differ in but minor details as **The Teachings of** to what the *Vedas* teach. We **the four Vedas :** may, therefore, safely say that they **1. The General** **Import.** give the knowledge of *Brahman*, and lay down work as a means to that knowledge. When through work (and by work is meant sacrificial rites as well as selfless labour) our hearts are purified, we become fit to inquire into the highest knowledge of *Brahman*.

The *Vedas* are accordingly divided into two parts— *Karma Kanda* devoted to work, and *Jnana Kanda,* devoted to knowledge. The *Upanishads,* the latter part of the *Vedas* (also called *Vedanta,* meaning ' the end of the *Vedas* '), comprise the section dealing with knowledge.

The *Karma Kanda* may be roughly divided into three parts : (*a*) the *Mantras* or hymns addressed in adoration of *Brahman* or God in His various aspects, a collection of these hymns being called *Samhita ;* (*b*) the Brahmanas written in prose describing the sacrificial rites and including precepts and religious duties; and (*c*) the *Aranyakas* or forest treatises which supplant the external rituals with symbolic meditations.

Professor Deussen has declared that this division of the *Vedas* is based on the principle of dividing life into *Ashramas* or stages of life. According to *Vedic* teachings, man's life has four stages. First is *Brahmacharya* or student life, when a boy lives with his teacher and receives both religious and secular instruction. The youth is trained in self-control and acquires such virtues as chastity, truth-fulness, faith and self-surrender. The next stage is *Garhasthya* or married life. The chief injunction for this stage is to practise the ritualistic sacrifices as explained in the *Brahmanas.* At the stage of retirement or *Vanaprastha*, he is no longer required to adhere to ritualism, but is enjoined to follow the *Aranyakas* or symbolic meditation. Finally he enters upon the life of renunciation, in which he is bound neither by work nor desire, but is dedicated wholly to acquiring the knowledge of *Brahman*.

Thus the general plan of life as taught in the *Vedas* is, successively, student life, married life, the life of retirement, and the life of renunciation. Each of these periods of a man's mortal existence has its special duties and observances, though it is also true that through a special *Vedic* declaration a person may enter immediately into the life of renunciation without passing through the intermediate stages of probation.

Through the institution of monasticism a man may enter early the life of renunciation. When one enters a monastery, he passes through a *Vedic* ritual while he meditates upon the truths of the *Upanishads*. According to *Vedic* teaching, this monastic life is the highest stage a man may attain. Modern India retains this ideal, and there are not wanting today men highly trained in Western science and literature who are willing to assume these monastic vows. Thus the influence of the *Vedas* has been perpetuated through the ages.

Parenthetically it may be said that the daily life and conduct of the people of India even today are guided by the injunctions of the *Vedas*. This is particularly true of the ceremonies connected with birth, marriage, and death. In the words of Professor Das Gupta, " The laws which regulate the social, legal, domestic and religious customs and rites of the Hindus even to the present day are said to be but mere systematized memories of old *Vedic* teachings, and are held to be obligatory on their authority." Every *Brahmin* repeats daily the *Vedic* prayer called the *Gayatri mantra,* which is a verse from the *Rig Veda.* It runs as follows :

Om bhur bhuvah swah tat savitur varenyam, bhargo devasya dhimahi, dhiyo yo nah prachodayat Om.

"May we meditate on the effulgent Light (or power) of Him who is worshipful, and who has given birth to all worlds. May He direct the rays of our intelligence towards the path of good."

V

The *Samhitas* form the first division of the work portion of the *Vedas.* They are collections of hymns sung in praise of the *Devas* or gods, the bright ones. These *Devas* are quite numerous in early *Vedic* literature, —Indra, Varuna, Mitra, Parjanya, and many others. These sometimes appear to be Nature gods, though again each one of them is also exalted and sublimated by the highest epithets of Godhead—that He is infinite, omnipresent, omnipotent, sees the hearts of all beings and so on. For example, Indra, one of the popular *Vedic* gods, possesses a body, is very strong, wears golden armour, and descends to earth where he lives and eats and with his votaries, fights their enemies, overcomes the demons, and establishes his

2. **The Samhitas.**

rule in heaven and upon earth. Another hymn tells how the whole universe exists in Indra, who is omnipotent and omnipresent. So also with Varuna, who is described as god of the air with control over the waters, but is also called omnipresent and omnipotent.

The following hymn [1] from the *Atharva Veda* addressed to the god Varuna gives utterance to this sublimation of his conception :

> The mighty Lord on high our deeds, as if at hand,
> espies ;
> The gods know all men do, though men would
> fain their deeds disguise.
> Whoever stands, whoever moves, or steals from
> place to place,
> Or hides him in his secret cell—the gods his
> movements trace.
> Wherever two together plot, and deem they are
> alone,
> King Varuna is there, a third, and all their
> schemes are known.
> This earth is his, to him belong those vast and
> boundless skies ;
> Both seas within him rest, and yet in that small
> pool he lies.
> Whoever far beyond the sky should think his way
> to wing,
> He could not there elude the grasp of Varuna
> the King.

[1] Translation by Muir.

His spies, descending from the skies, glide all the
    world around ;

Their thousand eyes all-scanning sweep to
    earth's remotest bound.

Whate'er exists in heaven and earth, whate'er
    beyond the skies,

Before the eyes of Varuna, the King, unfolded
    lies.

The ceaseless winkings all he counts of every
    mortal's eyes.

He wields this universal frame, as gamester
    throws his dice.

We thus find in the *Vedas* a peculiar situation.
While there is evidence that the outlook of the
primitive man, with his Nature worship and his
polytheism, is present, and hymns are addressed to
many gods, yet each of these gods is at times
sublimated into a single universal conception which
possesses the character of the infinite Personal
God of the universe. So does polytheism merge
into a monotheistic, though still anthropomorphic,
view of a Supreme God. Professor Max Muller
designates this process as henotheism.

The real explanation of this phenomenon, however, is to be found in the *Rig Veda,* " and it is a
grand explanation," declares Swami Vivekananda,
" one that has given the theme to all subsequent
thoughts in India, and one that will be the theme
of the whole world of religions—*Ekam sat vipra
bahudha vadanti.*—' (They call It Indra, Mitra,

Varuna :) That which exists is One, sages call It by various names."

Extraordinary results followed in India from this verse, for in it we find the germ of a universal religion. For this reason India has never known either religious fanaticism, or wars in the name of the gods. Through all the ages India has sought the truth in every religion ; not only does she tolerate other religions but she has an active sympathy for faiths not her own. Sri Ramakrishna in the modern age echoes this truth of universality when he says : " There is but one God, but endless are His names and endless the aspects in which He may be regarded. Call Him by any name, and worship Him in any aspect that pleases you ; you are sure to find Him. As many religions, so many paths to reach the same Truth. You will advance yourself in whatever way you may meditate upon Him or recite His holy name. The cake made with sugar-candy will taste equally sweet whether it be held straight or obliquely when you eat it."

Western *Vedic* scholars, in explaining the *Vedas*, are not ready to give up their theory of a gradual evolution of the conception of Godhead from simple Nature worship, through personification of the powers of Nature, to henotheism and the higher conception of monotheism. Whatever may have been the historical development of popular religious ideas, a Hindu brought up in the *Vedic* tradition finds no difficulty in realizing that even the earliest

Vedic seers were also worshipping the one God under various names ; for they knew that infinite is God and infinite are His expressions. Indra, Varuna, Mitra and others are as it were so many doors through which to enter into the inner being of the One Existence. *Ishtam,* the chosen ideal of Deity, is to a Hindu worshipper both the Supreme Being and He in whom the other gods reside.

The following famous hymn of the *Rig Veda* (X. 21) addressed to *Hiranyagarbha* gives expression to the conception of a Supreme Being :

" Before the universe became manifest, there was manifest *Hiranyagarbha.* He, being manifest, became the one lord of the manifested universe. He held within Himself the invisible world, the sky, and this earth. Unto Him who is *Ka*[1] we offer our sacrifice.

" He who is the purifier of our hearts, He who is the giver of strength, whose command all beings

[1] In the original Sanskrit there is the word *Kasmai* at the end of each verse. Professor Max Muller has translated the word as ' who is the god to whom we should offer our sacrifice ? ' And he has entitled the hymn as *Hymn to the Unknown God.* But Sayana renders the word differently. He declares that *Ka* means unknown ; that is, whose true being remains unknown and unknowable. Secondly, *Ka* denotes the one who desired the creation or manifestation of the universe. Third, the word means one who is the source of happiness. Thus these three renderings of the last sentence are possible :

(*a*) Unto Him whose being is unknown and unknowable, we offer our sacrifice.

(*b*) Unto Him who desired that this universe be created we offer our sacrifice.

(*c*) Unto Him who is the source of happiness we offer our sacrifice.

together with the gods obey, whose shadow is
immortality as well as mortality—unto Him, who
is *Ka,* we offer our sacrifice." [1]

The *Vedic* seers, however, did not stop with the
concept of a personal God. They realized that
whether they conceived Him as a God of revenge
or of justice, as a benevolent creator loving His
creatures or as *Ritasya Gopa,* the keeper and dis-
penser of physical and moral law and order, He
yet remained an anthropomorphic God. So these
bold *Vedic* thinkers are found asking, " Who has
seen the first born, when he that had no bones
(form and personality) bore him that has bones ?
Where is the life, the blood, the self of the universe ?
Who went to ask of any who knew ? " Swami
Vivekananda remarks of the *Vedic* seers, " The
monotheistic idea was much too human for them,
although they gave it such descriptions as—' The
whole universe rests on Him ', and ' Thou art the
keeper of all hearts '. The Hindus were, to their
great credit be it said, bold thinkers in all their
ideas, so bold that one spark of their thought
frightens the so-called bold thinkers of the present-
day world."

A creator, a ruler of the universe, is not his own
explanation ; and a God who is but an architect
does not satisfy man's insistent urge to understand
Him. Hence the *Vedic* seers continued to question,

[1] We have translated the above, following the commentary of Sayana.

and so we discover in various *Vedic* hymns answers formulated and poetically rendered. The following sublime hymn is such an answer :

" Then there was neither existence nor non-existence ; the world was not, nor the sky, nor anything beyond. Were there any of the subtle elements which by their appearance cover the reality behind ? Where would they exist ? And for whose experience ? Was there the deep fathomless abyss of water ?

" Then there was neither death nor deathlessness. Nor was there the knowledge of the distinction between night and day. That One, the source of light, existed without the motion of life. It existed united as one with its Power (*Maya*). Other than It, there was nothing.

" In the beginning there existed gloom hidden in gloom. This universe then remained undistinguished from its cause. This universe, which lay hidden in gloom, though it remained undistinguished, became manifested by the power of *Tapas* (the will of that One—the source of life and existence).

" Because in the heart there existed the seed, continued from the cycle of the previous universe, there arose the will. And the sages searching within themselves found the manifested existence hidden in the unmanifest.

" Who in reality knows and who can truly say how this creation came into existence and from what cause ? Even the *Devas* were born after the

creation came into existence. Hence who can know
the cause of this universe ?

" The source from which the universe sprang,
that alone can sustain it, none else. That One, the
lord of the universe, dwelling in Its own being,
undefiled as the sky above, alone knows the truth
of Its own creation, none else." [1]

Sayana, the great commentator, states that in
this hymn is brought out the truth that God is the
efficient as well as the material cause of the universe. Here also is found the advanced hypothesis
that the universe, which is without beginning or end
alternates between the phases of potentiality and
expression. This hymn is the source and authority
for a great deal of later philosophical speculation.

We have already seen that the *Vedic* seers did
not rest with the concept of a monotheistic God.
God in this hymn is described as *Tad Ekam*—That
One—neither masculine nor feminine, but neuter
' That '.

Another hymn, the famous *Purusha Sukta* of the
Rig Veda, attempts to express the inexpressible
nature of the infinite, impersonal, Absolute Truth.
It says :

" The Universal Being (the *Purusha*) has infinite
heads, un-numbered eyes, and un-numbered feet.
Enveloping the universe on every side, He exists
transcending it. All this is He—what has been

[1] *Rig Veda.* We have translated it following the commentary of Sayana.

and what shall be. He is the lord of immortality.
Though He has become all this, He is not all this
reality. For verily is He transcendental. The
whole series of universes (the past, present and
future) expresses His glory and power, but indeed
He transcends His own glory. All beings of the
universe form, as it were, a fraction of His Being.
But the rest of His Being is self-luminous and unchangeable. He who is beyond all predicates exists
as the relative universe. That part of His Being
coming within relativity, becomes extended as
sentient and insentient beings. From a part of Him
was born the body of the universe. Out of it were
born the gods, the earth, and men." [1]

In this hymn a definite rejection of pantheism is
made in the words, " Though He has become all
this, He is not all this in reality. For verily is He
transcendental."

But the conception of a Personal God still persists
in spite of the acceptance of an ideal of Godhead
which is impersonal and absolute. The truth is that
the infinite names, forms, attributes and expressions of God are but different ways of viewing a
single truth—That One Existence. *" Ekam Sat
vipra bahudha vadanti."*—" Truth is one ; sages
call It by various names." The Absolute is too
much of an abstraction to be loved, worshipped, or
meditated upon. It is to be realized by being or

---

[1] We have translated the hymn following the commentary of Sayana.

becoming It, and the process of that realization is worship and meditation upon It in Its personal aspect. " Personal God ", declares Swami Vivekananda, " is the reading of the Impersonal by the human mind." A Hindu, when taught to love and worship God, loves and worships Him as Personal-Impersonal.

In this connection, Max Muller says pertinently : " Whatever is the age when the collection of our *Rig Veda Samhita* was finished, it was before the age when the conviction was formed that there is but One, One Being, neither male nor female—a Being raised high above all the conditions and limitations of personality and of human nature, and, nevertheless, the Being that was really meant by all such names as Indra, Agni, Matarisvan, nay, even by the name of Prajapati, lord of creatures. In fact the *Vedic* poets had arrived at a conception of the Godhead which was reached once more by some of the Christian philosophers of Alexandria, but which even at present is beyond the reach of many who call themselves Christians."

VI

The second part of the work portion of the *Vedas* is called the *Brahmanas*. They are written in prose, and lay special emphasis upon sacrifices and sacrificial rites. " *Brahmana vividishanti yajnena danena*."—" The Brahmins desire to know, with the sacrifices and

3. **The Brahma-nas.**

charity as the means." That is, when the heart
becomes purified by the performance of sacrifices
and charity, there arises the hunger for the knowledge of Brahman. Thus is acknowledged the need
for the performance of sacrifices and the ceremonials
and rites of religion. But it is true that at times
undue importance was laid upon these rites as well
as on the mere chanting of the words of the *Vedas*,
so much so that the sacrifices themselves often took
the place of a living religion—a circumstance that
occurs in the development of all religious institutions.

Under such circumstances, prayer or supplication
before the object of worship becomes unnecessary ;
for by the performance of elaborate and fixed
sacrifices the gods may be forced to grant one's
desires. Professor Das Gupta believes that in these
sacrificial rites is to be found the germ of the law of
Karma, which the Hindu lawgiver Manu subse-
quently systematized philosophically in his code of
laws. "Thou canst not gather what thou dost not
sow. As thou dost sow, so wilt thou reap." [1]

This hardening of the institutional part of
religion exalted in time the power of the priests.
And it was in opposition to this externalizing and
crystallizing of what should have remained living
symbols of deeper truths behind appearances, and
also in opposition to the tyranny of a rising priest-
hood, that Buddha rose in revolt. The *Bhagavad*

[1] *Cf.* "Whatsoever a man soweth, that shall he also
reap." Gal. Ch. 6, V. 7.

Gita also condemns this tendency to attribute undue importance to ritualistic sacrifices.

Apart from the consideration of rituals, the *Brahmanas* lay emphasis upon duties and conduct as well. " Side by side with its insistence on the outer," writes S. Radhakrishnan, " there was also the emphasis on inner purity. Truth, godliness, honour to parents, kindness to animals, love of man, abstinence from theft, murder and adultery, were inculcated as the essentials of a good life." We find also certain injunctions which everyone must follow. The *Brahmanas* declare that we owe debts both to the world and to God, and certain duties must be discharged in repayment of these debts. These debts are mainly five, namely, those to the gods, to the *Rishis* or seers, to the *Pitris* or manes, to men, and to the lower creation. Our debt to the gods, we repay by performing the sacrifices ; to the seers, by feeling devotion in our hearts for their greatness ; to the manes, by praying for them ; to men, by feeling love and sympathy and by doing kind deeds ; and to the lower creation, by offering them food and drink. When we partake of our daily meals, we must offer parts of it regularly to gods, manes, men and animals, accompanied by proper prayers. These are debts and must be paid. No merit is therefore acquired by their observance ; on the other hand, by neglecting them, we degenerate below the worth of a human being. These duties enjoined in the *Brahmanas* must not be performed for the purpose of gaining selfish ends. They are to be gone through for the sake of purifying the heart and as the obligatory duty of a righteous man.

VII

The *Aranyakas,* which form the third part of the *Vedas,* regard the various rites
4. The Aranyakas. explained in the *Brahmanas* as but symbols for meditation. They lay far greater stress upon retiring into one's own self than upon the intrinsic value of external acts. Swami Vivekananda explains the change in these words :

" Thus we find that the minds of these ancient Aryan thinkers had begun a new theme. They found out that in the external world no search would give an answer to their question. So they fell back upon this other method, and according to this they were taught that these desires of the senses, desire for ceremonials and externalities, have caused a veil to come between themselves and the truth, and that this cannot be removed by any ceremonial. . . . they seemed to declare—look not for the truth in any religion ; it is here in the human soul, the miracle of all miracles—in the human soul, the emporium of all knowledge, the mine of all existence—. . . and they found out step by step that that which is external is but a dull reflection at best of that which is inside . . . Just at first it was a search after the *Devas,* the bright ones, and then it was the origin of the universe, and the very same search is getting another name more philosophical, clearer,—the unity of all things, " knowing which everything else becomes known '."[1]

[1] The Complete Works—Vol.   pp. 354-355.

CHAPTER III

THE PHILOSOPHY OF THE UPANISHADS

I

THE *Upanishads* form the concluding portion of
the *Vedas*. They are also called
What are the the *Vedanta,* the *anta,* or end of
Upanishads ? the *Vedas,* that is, the highest
wisdom. Although one hundred and eight of them
have been preserved, ten of them alone have been
commented upon by the great *Vedantist* Samkara
(686 A.D.), and have, as a consequence, become the
principal source for the study of Hindu religion.[1]

The exact date of their composition is not known,
but the most authoritative opinion assigns the
earliest of them to a period between 3000 B.C. and
800 B.C. Some of the most important manuscripts
are dated about 500 B.C., some years later than the
age of Buddha. Their authorship, if individual
authorship there was, is also unknown, and the
tradition concerning the origin of the early *Vedas*
persists with respect to these later scriptures also.

[1] These ten are *Isa, Kena, Katha, Prasna, Mundaka,
Mandukya, Chandogya, Brihadaranyaka, Aitareya,* and
Taittiriya.

The word *Upanishad* means literally 'sitting near devotedly', (*upa*, near ; *ni*, devotedly ; *shad*, sitting). The word is also used in the further sense of 'secret teachings'. Samkara derives a third meaning from the word, *viz.*, the knowledge of *Brahman* ; for such knowledge destroys the bonds of ignorance and leads to the supreme goal of freedom. All the three of these meanings can, in fact, be derived from the word ; for this highest wisdom can be learned by sitting devotedly at the feet of a teacher who himself possesses it and embodies it in life, and communicates the same to the world at large through secret channels—that is, imparts it only to those who have attained purity of heart through previous self-discipline.

The great *importance* of the Upanishads in religious history has been recognized by scholars the world over. The famous German Orientalist, Deussen, gives utterance to this fact in these words : " The sparks of philosophic light appearing in the *Rig Veda,* shine out brighter and brighter until at last in the *Upanishads* they burst into that bright flame which is able to light and warm us today." One great modern philosopher, whose inspiration came largely from the study of Indian philosophy, has also given testimony to the universal appeal of these early expressions of religious insight. Schopenhauer declares : " From every sentence deep, original and sublime thoughts arise, and the whole is pervaded by a high and holy and earnest spirit. . . . .

In the whole world there is no study, except that of the originals, so beneficial and so elevating as that of the *Oupanikhat* (the Persian word for *Upanishad*). It has been the solace of my life, it will be the solace of my death."

The *Upanishads* do, indeed, reveal to us in exalted and sublime language the central fact of religion, the mystery of the ultimate reality, as they record the direct perception of the *Rishis* of early ages— the truths concerning God, man and the universe. These are the same truths that have been revealed to specially endowed spiritual leaders in every age, and that can be rediscovered by every individual who aspires for his own soul's liberation. They form the original source of the great religions of the world.

The *Rishis,* who gave utterance to these revelations, remain wholly in the background. We know nothing of their personal lives. They remain as impersonal as the truths which they realized and gave forth to be the possession of all humanity.

In no sense are these writings a systematic exposition of any particular doctrine, but they are rather revelations and outpourings from inspired souls. Many later philosophers, it is true, have attempted to derive from them a systematic doctrine and a unified revelation. Of these, Samkara (686 A.D.), the champion of *Advaita Vedanta,* and Ramanuja (1017-1137 A.D.), the founder of the qualified monistic school of *Vedanta,* are among the most

important. Both of these philosophers have unques-
tionably found support for their schools of thought
in certain of the texts. Especially is this the case
with Samkara's school ; for, as we have already
noted, his commentary is concerned with ten of the
greatest *Upanishads*. But whatever philosophical
theory or world-view may be derived from a partial
reading of these great religious documents, the
fundamental fact remains that they stand essentially
as a witness of an unchangeable reality behind the
universe of change, and of the fact of this reality
being identical with the reality within man. The
Upanishads invariably give the name *Atman* to this
reality within, which is identical with *Brahman* or
reality behind the universe. The teachings of these
books do, in fact, distinctly lead us, in our quest for
truth, from the external world to a search within
ourselves. In the words of the *Katha Upanishad*,
" God created the senses outgoing. Hence man
experiences the external world and sees not the
Inner Self. Some who are wise, wishing immortality, control those outgoing senses and find the
Self within."

II

These two words, *'Brahman'* and *'Atman'*, are,

**Brahman and
Atman.**

as it were, ' the two pillars on
which rests the whole edifice of
Indian philosophy '. They are,
respectively, the objective and the subjective views

of the reality behind the world of appearances which is the constant theme of these early religious writings. In *Brahman* we find something, of which this changing world is but a partial and incomplete expression ; It is the source and sustenance of the universe. Says the *Taittiriya Upanishad,* " That from which all these beings are born, and in which, being born, they live, and into which they all enter after dissolution—seek to know That. That is *Brahman.*"

Brahman, as the source of all power, such as of fire to burn, of water to drench, and of the senses of man to work, is explained allegorically in the *Kena Upanishad.* In contrast to this, Its transcendental nature has thus been described in the *Brihadaranyaka Upanishad* : " This is the *Brahman,* without cause and without effect, without anything inside or outside."

He is both transcendent and immanent, and this latter quality of immanence, the *Mundaka Upanishad* explains in the following words : " Formless, that self-luminous Being exists within and without, higher than the highest. From Him issue life, and mind, and senses—ether, air, water, fire, and the earth. Heaven is his head, the moon and the sun are His eyes, the quarters His ears, the revealed *Vedas* His speech. His breath is the air, the universe is His heart, and the earth touches His feet. He is the innermost Self in all beings. He who knows Him hidden in the shrine of his heart cuts the knot of ignorance even in this life. Self-luminous, ever present in the hearts of all, is the great Being. He is the refuge of all. In Him exists all that moves and breathes. Adorable is He. He is the supreme goal. He is beyond the known, and beyond the knowable. He is self-luminous, subtler than the subtlest; in Him exist all the worlds and those that live therein. He is that imperishable *Brahman*. He is the life-principle; He is the speech and the mind; He is the truth; He is immortal. He is to be realized. Attain Him, O friend."

But *Brahman* is also indefinable, predicateless. How, then, can these opposing attributes be reconciled? In the words of the *Taittiriya Upanishad, Brahman* is He 'whom speech cannot express and from whom the mind comes away baffled, unable to reach'. Samkara's commentary upon the aphorisms of *Vedanta* tells, in reference to an *Upanishad* no longer extant, of a student approaching a Master to learn of *Brahman*. "Sir, teach me the nature of *Brahman*," he requested. The Master did not reply. When he was importuned a second and a third time, he answered, " I teach you indeed, but you do not follow. His name is silence." Says the *Kena Upanishad* describing *Brahman* : " That which cannot be expressed by speech, but which illumines speech, know that to be *Brahman*. That which cannot be conceived by mind, but by which mind thinks, know that to be *Brahman*. That which is not visible to the eye, but by which the eye sees, know that to be *Brahman*. That which is not heard by the ear, but by which the ear hears, know that to be *Brahman*. That which is not breathed, but by which the breath functions, know that to be *Brahman*."

Brahman, then, was the name given by the Rishin to the unchanging reality in this external universe. But this *Brahman* remains a mere abstraction unless It becomes known to us through realization, and we become It. We read in the *Upanishads* how, when the quest for knowledge of *Brahman* is pushed to its furthermost limit, it eventually ends by the inquirer seeing the *Brahman* within his own Self. Only thus does the abstraction become a reality, and the hypothesis assumes the character of certitude. *Atman* signifies this self in man, the self which is not limited in Itself but, in the words of the *Katha Upanishad,* is subtler than the subtle, greater than the great, and is dwelling in the hearts of all. As fire, being one, assumes different forms according to what it burns, so the *Atman* existing in all, though one, assumes different forms according to whatever It enters. It also exists without.

Deussen truly remarks, " It was here that for the first time, the original thinkers of the *Upanishads,* to their immortal honour, found It when they recognized one *Atman,* one inmost individual being, as the *Brahman*, the inmost being of universal Nature and of all her *phenomena*."

Brahman and *Atman,* and indeed the whole teaching of the Upanishads, are revealed with a fair degree of completeness in the Great Sayings[1] or the *Mahavakyas,* such as *Tat tvam asi* (Thou art That) ; *Aham Brahmasmi* (I am *Brahman*) ; *Soham asmi* (I am He) ; and so on.

There is preserved in the *Chandogya Upanishad,* a dialogue between a certain Uddalaka and his son, Svetaketu, which helps to make clear the meaning and implication of the Great Saying *Tat tvam asi* or ' Thou art That '. When Svetaketu was twelve years old, so runs the tale, his father Uddalaka said to him, " Svetaketu, you must now go to school to study. None of our family, darling, is ignorant of *Brahman.*" Thereupon Svetaketu went to a teacher and studied for twelve years. Then, after learning all the *Vedas,* he returned home and was full of pride in his learning. His father, noticing the boy's conceit, asked him : " Svetaketu, my child, have you asked for that knowledge by which we hear the unhearable, by which we perceive the

[1] These Great Sayings or *Mahavakyas,* which bring out the identity of *Brahman* and *Atman,* are found in different places in the *Upanishads.* It would be of interest to note in this connection, that the *Sannyasins* or monks of the school of Samkara, who are divided into ten classes, receive one of these *Mahavakyas* from a competent teacher during the time of initiation into monkhood. The disciple must then meditate on the *Mahavakya* and realize *Brahman* as identical with the inner Self. The different classes of monks are differentiated according to the particular Mahavakya they receive in their particular Orders.

4

unperceivable, by which we know the unknowable ? "
" What is that knowledge, sir ? " asked Svetaketu.
The father replied : " My dear, as by knowing one
lump of clay, all that is made of clay is known,
the difference being only in name, and the truth
being that all is clay ; as by knowing a nugget
of gold, all that is made of gold is known, the
difference being only in name, and the truth being
that all is gold,—so, my child, is that knowledge,
knowing which we know everything." The son
replied :   " Surely those venerable teachers of
mine do not know this knowledge ; for if they had
knowledge of it, they would have taught it to me.
Do you, sir, therefore, impart that knowledge to
me." " Be it so," said the father. " Believe, my
child, that That which is the subtle essence, in That
has all its existence. That is the True, That is the
Self ; and thou art That, O Svetaketu." " Please,
sir, tell me more about this Self," said the son. " So
be it, my child," replied the father. " Put this salt
in water, and come to me tomorrow morning."
The son did as he was told.

The next morning the father asked the boy to
bring him the salt which he had put into the water.
But he could not, for it had dissolved. The father
said, " Sip the water and tell me how it tastes."
" It is salty, sir," replied the son. Then the father
said, " In the same way, though you do not perceive
the True, there indeed is That. That which is the
subtle essence, in That has all this its existence,

That is the True ; That is the Self ; and thou art That, O Svetaketu."

"Please, sir, tell me more about this Self," requested Svetaketu. "So be it, my child," the father said. "As a bee, O Svetaketu, gathers honey from different flowers, and as the different drops of honey do not know that they are from different flowers, so all of us, having come to that existence, know not that we have done so. And as the rivers, when they become one with the ocean, do not know that they have been various rivers, even so when we come out of that existence, we do not know that we are That. Now That which is the subtle essence, in It is the True. It is the Self ; and thou, O Svetaketu, art That."

"Please, sir, tell me more about this Self," said the son again. "So be it, my child," replied the father. "As a person might be blindfolded and led away from his home and left in a strange place ; and as he would turn in every direction and cry for someone to remove his bandages and show him the way home ; and as someone might loosen the bandages and show him the way ; and as thereupon he would walk, asking his way from village to village as he went, and arrive at his home at last,—in exactly the same manner does a man who meets with an illumined teacher, obtain the true knowledge. That which is the subtle essence, in That has all this its existence. That is the True ; That is the Self ; and thou art That, O Svetaketu."

III

In this dialogue between Uddalaka and his son,
Svetaketu, we learn, "That which
Thou art That.   is the subtle essence, in That has
all this its existence, and That which is *Sat*
—Existence itself—That thou art." This, then,
is the fundamental truth of the philosophy
of the *Upanishads*—the identity between *Brahman*
and *Atman,* between God and man. To a
superficial reader who fails to penetrate deep into
the mystery of man's soul, this doctrine of identity
may easily become the ground for misconceptions
and misinterpretations. But the *Upanishads* give us
that profounder analysis of the essential nature of
man, which the people of the Western world seem
to have missed—an analysis which affords a
convincing explanation of the identity of the Spirit
in man with God.

According to this account of human nature, man,
in the form in which he is known to his fellows, is
called *Jiva*—he who breathes—denoting the biologi-
cal and physiological aspects of his life. His
individual self is further indicated by the words,
Bhokta, meaning the experiencer, the enjoyer ; and
Karta, meaning the doer. "For he it is," says the
Prasna Upanishad, "who sees, hears, smells, tastes,
perceives, conceives, acts,—he whose essence is
knowledge, the Person who dwells in the highest,
indestructible Self." Again, in the words of the

Katha Upanishad, "When the Self is in union with the body, the senses, and the mind, then wise people call him enjoyer."

These quotations have reference to the psychological or conscious aspect of life. So man is the Self associated with *Prana*—the vital principle or that which expresses itself as breath—and with *Manas,* which comprises mind, intelligence and ego. In addition to these there are also the physical body and the organs of the senses. These *Indriyas* or sense organs are, according to the *Upanishads,* ten in number, five known as the senses of knowledge, *i.e.,* the organs of sight, hearing, touch, smell, and flavour (taste) ; and five senses of action, namely, the organs of speech, holding, moving, excretion and generation.

Says the *Taittiriya Upanishad,* in its detailed analysis of man : " This Self is covered over by ' sheaths ' as it were. First is the physical sheath, this body, which is made up of the essence of food. Therefore it is called *Annamaya,* or composed of food. Different from this is another more subtle sheath of the Self, which is made of *Prana,* the life principle. Like the shape of the former is the human shape of the latter, even as water which assumes the shape of the vessel into which it is poured. It is known as *Pranamaya,* inasmuch as it is constituted of *Prana,* which manifests as energy. Different from this is the *Manomaya* sheath, which is made up of *Manas,* mind. It is also like unto the shape of the man. Different from this, which is made up of *Manas,* is the other sheath, which is made up of *Vijnana* or intelligence. And different from this is the other, which is made up of ego. It is called *Anandamaya,* the sheath of bliss : for it is the innermost covering of the blissful Self."

These sheaths cover the Self. Since the true Self is one with *Brahman,* it can be none of these sheaths, nor can Its nature be known so long as It is identified in our consciousness with one or all of them. Hence the *Katha Upanishad* says, "Know the body to be the chariot, the intellect the charioteer, the mind the reins, and the *Atman* the lord of the chariot."

But what proof have we of an *Atman* distinct from the mind, the intelligence, the ego and the body ? Western philosophy declares mind and soul to be identical, with nothing existing behind the mind and the ego. But in the *Upanishads* this something behind the changing forms of our lives is declared to exist, and no need is felt for proofs of any sort. For the Self is the basis of all proofs, and so stands in need of none. In the words of the *Brihadaranyaka Upanishad,* "That by which one knows all this—whereby could one know That ? By what means could the Knower be known ? ".

All this, of course, is not tantamount to agnosticism. We find again and again the injunction to 'know thyself', to seek to 'know the knower', 'to seek to know, not the object seen, but the seer of objects '.

The fact is that the existence of the *Atman* is self-evident, since It is the ' eternal witness ', the ' eternal subject ', the ' unchangeable reality ' in man. There is indeed a simple argument implicit in the utterances of these seers, and this has been brought to light by later philosophers. To state it briefly, motion or change can be known only in relation to something that is comparatively static. The movement of this, in turn, must be known in relation to a third object moving still slower, and so on *ad infinitum*, until one arrives at something absolutely beyond all motion and change. Body, mind, everything we experience, is a series of changes. There must, therefore, be something beyond them which does not change. Moreover, the subject or the witness cannot be an object seen or cognized ; and our minds, egos, senses, bodies, etc., as the instruments of knowledge, are only cognized objects. They cannot, therefore, be the subject or the witness. So there must be a separate something, the *Atman,* which is the eternal witness, the eternal subject.

When the *Atman* identifies Itself with the sheaths, it appears as *Jiva,* an individual man. How this identification has come about is an interesting problem in later philosophies. The *Upanishads* declare that *Jivahood* has been effected by the forgetfulness of the *Atman,* and the loss of its essential identity with *Brahman.* Samkara, in the Introduction to his commentary on the *Vedanta* aphorisms, considers the problem of how the *Atman* identifies itself with its sheaths, the non-self. This, he says, is caused by *Avidya* or ignorance. He points out that the subject is the Self whose nature is intelligence, and the object is the non-self. They are opposed to each other as darkness is to light, and so they cannot be identified, much less their respective attributes. And it is wrong to superimpose upon the subject, the object or its attributes. Yet, through some unexplainable cause that has its root in ignorance, man, from a beginningless past, fails to distinguish between the two and their respective attributes, although they are absolutely distinct, and would " superimpose upon each the characteristic nature and the attributes of the other, thus coupling the real and the unreal. . . . Extrapersonal attributes are superimposed on the Self if a man considers himself sound and entire, or the contrary, as long as his wife, children and so on are sound and entire or not. Attributes of the body are superimposed on the Self, if a man thinks of himself (his Self) as stout, lean, fair, as standing, walking or jumping. Attributes of the sense-organs, if he thinks, ' I am mute, or deaf, or one-eyed, or blind '. Attributes of the internal organs, when he considers himself subject to desire, intention, doubt, determination, and so on. . . . In this way there goes on this natural beginning—and endless superimposition, which appears in the form of wrong conception, is the cause of individual souls appearing as agents and enjoyers (of the results of their actions), and is observed by every one." [1]

In this connection, Swami Vivekananda relates the following interesting story : " There was once a baby lion left by its dying mother among some sheep. The sheep fed it and gave it shelter. The lion grew apace and said ' Ba-a-a ' when the sheep said ' Ba-a-a '. One day another lion came by. ' What do you do here ? ' said the second lion in astonishment, for he heard the sheep-lion bleating with the rest. ' Ba-a-a,' said the other, ' I am a little sheep, I am a little sheep, I am frightened.' ' Nonsense ! ' roared the second lion. ' Come with me ; I will show you your true nature ! ' And he took him to the side of a smooth stream and showed him his own image therein. ' You are a lion ; look at me, look at the sheep, look at yourself.' And the sheep-lion looked, and then he said, ' Ba—I do not look like the sheep, it is true. I am a lion ! ' and with that he roared a roar that shook the hills to their depths. That is it. We are lions in sheep's clothing of habit, we are hypnotized into weakness by our surroundings, and the province of *Vedanta* is the de-hypnotization of the Self."

A beautiful allegory is related in the *Mundaka Upanishad* to illustrate this point. " Like two birds of beautiful golden plumage—inseparable companions

[1] From G. Thibaut's translation of Samkara's *Sutra Bhashya*.

—the *Jivatman* (the individual self) and the *Para-matman* (the Universal Self) are perched on the branches of the self-same tree. Of those, the one (the individual self) tastes of the sweet and bitter fruits of the tree, and the other (the Universal Self) remains motionless, calmly observing. Though living on the self-same tree, the individual self, deluded by the forgetfulness of its divine nature, grieves, bewildered by its own helplessness. And when the same one recognizes the worshipful Lord as its own true Self, and beholds His glory, it becomes free from all grief. Thus, when the individual realizes the self-luminous Lord, the cause of all causes, it sheds all impurities and realises its identity with the Universal Self."

In the *Chandogya Upanishad* the question regarding the essential nature of man or the Self, is discussed in the tale of Indra and Virochana who approached the teacher Prajapati to gain the knowledge of the Self. Prajapati commences his instruction with an indication of the nature of the Self. " That Self which is free from impurities, free from old age or death, from hunger or thirst, whose desire is true and whose desires come true, that Self is to be sought after, that Self is to be enquired about and realized. He who, learning about his Self, realizes Him, obtains all the worlds and all desires."

Students of logic may condemn this tendency to assume that the Self is self-evident and true, on the ground that one takes for granted what one is required to prove. Deeper reflection on the subject however, would convince one that, after all, it is not so illogical. We have already seen how, logically, we must accept the existence of an unchanging reality. In virtue of its unchangeability, this reality is free from impurities, old age, and death, which are the attributes of the mind and the body alone, and not of the Self. So the Self in Itself must not only be unchangeable, but pure, free and immortal.

Now in the story we are told that Indra from among the *Devas* or gods, and Virochana from among the *Asuras* or demons, approached Prajapati, and after having served him for thirty-two years, begged of him to teach them the knowledge of the Self. Prajapati replied to them : "The Person that is seen in the eye, that is the Self. That is immortal, That is fearless, and That is *Brahman*." Then they asked, "Sir, is he the Self who is seen reflected in the water or in a mirror?" Prajapati gave a clear reply that they might inquire further. He said, "He, the Atman, indeed, is seen in all these. Look at your own self in the water, and whatever you do not understand, come and tell me."

They looked at their reflections in water, and when asked what they had seen of the Self, they replied, "Sir, we see the Self, we see even the hair and nails." Then Prajapati bade them don their finest clothes and look again at their 'selves' in the water. This they did, and when asked what they had seen, they replied : "We see the Self, just as we are, well

adorned and in our finest clothes." Prajapati said
then, "The Self indeed is seen in these. That Self
is immortal, fearless, and That is *Brahman*."

And they went away, pleased at heart. But
Prajapati, looking after them, said, "Both of them
departed without analysing or discriminating, and
without comprehending the true Self. And whoever
will follow this false doctrine of the Self will perish."

Now Virochana, satisfied that he had known the
Self, returned to the *Asuras* and preached the
doctrine of the body as Self. But Indra, on his way
back, realized the uselessness of this knowledge. So
he thought within himself, "As this Self seems to
be well adorned when the body is well adorned,
well dressed when the body is well dressed, so will
this Self be blind if the body is blind, lame if the
body is lame, deformed if the body is deformed—
in fact, this Self will die also when the body perishes.
I see no good in such knowledge." So he returned
to Prajapati and asked for further instruction.
Prajapati said, "He who moves about in dreams,
enjoying and glorified, he is the Self. That is
immortal, fearless, and That is *Brahman*."

Pleased at heart, Indra again departed. But
before he had returned to the *Devas,* he realized
the uselessness of that Knowledge also. He thought
within himself : "True it is that this Self is not
blind if the body is blind ; nor lame, nor hurt
if the body is lame or hurt. But in dreams, too, this
Self is conscious of many sufferings. So I see no

good in this teaching."

Thus Prajapati takes his disciple step by step
through the long process of thinking for himself.
From the realization that the body cannot be the
free, immortal, unchanging Self, Indra now turns to
analyse the dream self. For in dreams one attains
to a purer state of mind, in so far as one experiences
objects through means other than the body and the
senses. In a way the dream self is above the physical
self. But the disciple soon discovered that this also
could not be the true Self. And he again approached
Prajapati for further instruction on the matter.
Prajapati then said, " When a person is asleep,
reposing and at perfect rest, dreaming no dreams,
then he realises the Self. That is immortal and
fearless, and That is *Brahman.*" Satisfied, Indra
went away. But even before he had reached home,
he felt the uselessness of this knowledge. " In
reality," thought he, " one does not know oneself as,
' This is I ', while asleep. One is not, in fact,
conscious of any existence. That state is almost annihilation. I see no good in this knowledge either."

Sir S. Radhakrishnan comments on this statement
thus : " Indra was too much of a psychologist for
Prajapati. He felt that this Self, freed from all
bodily experience, from the shapeless mass of
dreams, etc., is an objectless and barren fiction.
. . . Peel off layer after layer of an onion, and what
remains ? Nothing. Bradley points out : ' The ego
that pretends to be anything either before or beyond

its concrete psychical filling is a gross fiction and a mere monster, and for no purpose admissible. On this view, in dreamless sleep there is no self at all. Locke declares that every drowsy nod explodes the self theory. 'In sleep and trances the mind exists not—there is no time, no succession of ideas. To say the mind exists without thinking is a contradiction' (Berkeley's Works, Vol. 1, p. 34). Indra seems to have been an empiricist ages before Locke and Berkeley. 'If the soul in a perfectly dreamless sleep thinks, feels and wills nothing, is the soul then at all, and if it is, how is it?' asks Locke. 'How often has the answer been given, that if this could happen, the soul would have no being? Why have we not the courage to say, that, as often as this happens, the soul is not?' Indra has the courage to declare it. It is indeed destroyed."[1]

To explain to Indra that the mind is not the Self, because the Self continues to exist without the mind, Prajapati wished his disciple to analyse the state of deep sleep. And Indra, who had identified the mind with the Self through ignorance, discovered that he had not known the Self; for mind is 'almost annihilated' in dreamless sleep. It is a conclusion similar to that of Western rationalists like Bradley, Locke, and Berkeley. But these philosophers failed to inquire further, and remained satisfied with their conclusion—"To say that the mind exists without

[1] *The Philosophy of the Upanishads,* by S. Radhakrishnan, pp. 31-2.

thinking is a contradiction, nonsense, nothing." Indra became so much dissatisfied that he sought to know the Self beyond the mind. For though the mind exists not in deep sleep, it being contentless and objectless then, there must continue to exist something which holds our experiences before and after sleep. This persisting entity is the unchangeable reality, the Self. S. Radhakrishnan rightly remarks, however, " Devadatta, after good sleep, continues to be Devadatta, since his experiences unite themselves to the system which existed at the time when he went to sleep. They link themselves to his thoughts and do not fly to any other's. This continuity of experience requires us to admit a permanent self underlying all contents of consciousness."

Indra approached his teacher Prajapati once more and asked to be taught. And this time Prajapati gave him the highest truth of the Self. He said : " This body is mortal, always gripped by death. But herein resides the immortal Self, formless. This Self, when associated in consciousness with the body (the different sheaths), becomes subject to pleasure and pain. As long as there is the association with the body, no one is free from the dual throng of pleasure and pain. But as one becomes free from this association and body consciousness, no pleasure or pain can touch or affect the Self. Rising above physical consciousness, and knowing the Self as distinct from the senses, sense-organs and the mind, knowing Him in His true light, one rejoices and is free. He who knows that Self, and meditates and realizes that Self obtains all worlds and all desires."

IV

The *Mandukya Upanishad* refers to three states of consciousness, and to a Fourth, which may be termed transcendental consciousness. From the standpoint of the *Jiva* each state is given a name. From the standpoint of *Brahman* also four corresponding aspects are conceived. The first is the waking state, which is known as *Vaisvanara*. It is characterised by the awareness of things outside, the enjoyment of gross objects with the senses, and the feeling of identification of consciousness with the physical body. This we may call the individual aspect of man. When we consider the universal aspect of *Brahman* as the physical world parallel to this state of individual consciousness, we call it *Virat* or the Cosmos. It is the totality of all existence : " Heaven is His head, the moon and the sun are His eyes, the quarters His ears, the revealed *Vedas* His speech, the air His breath, and the universe His heart. The earth touches His feet." Of the *Virat* or Cosmos, the individual being or *Vaisvanara* is a part.

The second is the dreaming state. This aspect of consciousness in the individual is known as *Taijasa*. It is aware of internal objects and enjoys mental impressions. This is the intermediate state

Study of Consciousness.

between waking and deep sleep. The mind is now
active without the use of the sense-organs and is
devoid of consciousness of the gross body. Man now
becomes a mental being. In the universal aspect,
corresponding to this state of individual consciousness, *Brahman* is known as *Hiranyagarbha,* or
sometimes simply *Brahma,* the first born of God—
the effect God—as distinguished from *Isvara*, the
causal God. *Hiranyagarbha* is the cosmic mind, and
our individual minds are parts of this universal mind.

The third of these states is deep sleep, in which
consciousness is known as *Prajna*. Here, there is
cessation of all awareness of the external world, and
besides, the mind's self-consciousness ' appears to
be unified under the pall of gloom, and is said to
be of the form of bliss '. Man is now free from
physical consciousness, and the mind is negated as
well. We have now reached the veil of ego, the
causal sheath, so named because the root of all
consciousness is in the ' sheath ' of ego. Corresponding to it, in the universal aspect, is *Isvara*
or God, the creator of all beings and all things.
This *Isvara* is the Personal God of the Hindus,
defined as *Brahman* in association with *Maya* or
universal ignorance. But it must be understood
that, though *Isvara* is the Lord of *Maya*, He is not
in any manner affected by *Maya*. In contrast to
Isvara, Jiva or man is *Brahman* associated with
Avidya, individual ignorance, and is bound by it.
Isvara, or *Brahman* in His personal aspect, is the

5

object of adoration for the devout, who at the same time know that He is the Soul of their souls, dwelling within the shrine of their hearts.

The *Turiya,* which means the Fourth, is the transcendental consciousness. This *Turiya* is identical with pure *Atman.* The *Mandukya Upanishad* describes it thus : " That which is not conscious of internal objects, nor of external objects, nor of objects in the intermediary state, and is not a negative consciousness ; which is neither conscious nor unconscious ; which is unrelated, unperceivable, beyond all connotations, beyond all thought, indefinable, whose nature is pure self-consciousness, beyond relative existence ; which is peaceful, of blissful nature and is the One without a second— that the wise call *Turiya,* the Fourth. That is the Self. He is to be realized." Here there is neither individual aspect nor universal aspect. *Atman* is *Brahman.*—" Thou art That ".[1]

---

[1] The following table will be helpful in understanding the relationship of the states of consciousness, and their various expressions in their individual and universal aspects :

	INDIVIDUAL	UNIVERSAL
1. Waking ..	*Vaisvanara* or physical consciousness	*Virat* or Cosmos
2. Dream ..	*Taijasa* or subtle body (mind)	*Hiranyagarbha,* the Effect God
3. Sleep ..	*Prajna* or causal sheath (ego body)	*Isvara* or *Brahman* and *Maya* : (but Lord of *Maya*)

4. *Turiya* or *Atman-Brahman* as set forth in the Great Saying ' Thou art That '.

V

In the teachings of the *Upanishads,* the doctrine of identity of *Brahman*

Cosmic and Acosmic Ideals. with *Atman* assumes two distinct forms following two different trends of thought. The first of them is *Saprapancha* or cosmic, and identifies *Brahman* not only with the *Atman* but with the Cosmos. The second is *Nish-prapancha* or acosmic, as it negates the Cosmos and lays stress on the oneness of *Brahman* and *Atman* in the transcendental state. To these two views may be added a third—one merely suggested in the *Upanishads*—that this *Brahman* or *Atman* is

In this connection it may be pointed out that *Vedanta* has three schools of thought, all finding their authority in the *Vedas*. The main distinction between them centres round the problem of the relation of man to God. The *Dvaita,* or dualist school expounded by Madhva, believes in man and God as eternally separate, related as created being and Creator. The *Visishtadvaita* school, expounded by Ramanuja, believes in one Universal Totality, a Whole, and man is a part of the Whole. There is unity in differ-ence. The *Advaita* school, expounded by Samkara, be-lieves in the complete identity of *Atman* with *Brahman.* The *Upanishads,* on the whole, support the philosophy of Samkara.

Sri Ramakrishna harmonises the different schools by quoting an old Sanskrit verse, " When I have the cons-ciousness that I am the body, I am Thy servant and Thou art my Lord. When I identify myself as the individual soul, Thou art the Whole and I am Thy part. And when I know my true Self, I am one with Thee." And the high-est truth is this identity.

Christ also seems to have had the same idea in view when at one time he prayed to the " Father in Heaven ". Then again he says, " I am the vine, ye are the branches." And the highest truth is taught when he declares, " I and my Father are one."

indefinable and inexpressible.   *Upasantoyamatma.*—
" Silence is His name."

Concerning *Saprapancha,* the first of these
aspects, the *Chandogya Upanishad* tells us that
Brahman is ' He who gives birth to this world,
who supports it and re-absorbs it—whose body is
spirit, whose form is light, whose thoughts are true,
who pervades all and is the living presence in all
and everything '. And the Self or *Atman,* it is
stated, is subtler than the subtle and greater than
the great, and dwells within the heart, and is
identical with *Brahman.*

A famous dialogue between Yajnavalkya and his
wife Maitreyi, to be found in the *Brihadaranyaka
Upanishad,* explains the way in which the one
Self pervades everything in the universe, dwells in
the body of man, and expresses Itself as the life of
all beings. " This world, which is so sweet to all
beings, and to which every being is so sweet, is but
the Self-effulgent. The Immortal is the bliss in the
world. In us also He is that bliss. He is *Brahman.*"
The Self or *Brahman* is the essence, the reality,
behind this universe. Having created this world out
of Himself, He again enters into it. " From *Ananda*
or joy springs this universe ; in joy it has its being,
and unto joy it returns."

The all-pervading nature of *Brahman* is expressed
in this exquisite passage from the *Svetasvatara Upanishad* : " Thou art woman ; Thou art man ; Thou
art the youth and maiden too ; Thou as an old man

art tottering with Thy staff. Thou existeth everywhere.
Thou art the dark blue insect. Thou art the green
parrot with red eyes. Thou art the thunder cloud.
Thou art the seasons. Thou art without beginning.
Thou art all-pervading. From Thee has come forth the
whole universe."

On such passages as these, has the philosopher
Ramanuja based his doctrine of transformation
(*Parinamavada*). The world, he declares, is not
separate from God, but God has transformed Himself as this world. But in so doing, He has not
exhausted Himself, nor is He affected in any way.
Thus in the *Upanishads* we hear this truth :

> Filled with *Brahman* are the things we sense ;
> Filled with *Brahman* are the things we sense not ;
> From out of *Brahman* floweth all that is,
> From *Brahman* all, yet is He still the same.

Before discussing *Nishprapancha,* the second of
these aspects of identity between *Brahman* and
Atman, it may be well to summarize the principles
to be derived from such passages as we have quoted
above.

1. *Brahman* is one with Atman, is the essence,
the reality, behind the changing phenomena of the
universe. He pervades it in the sense that He is
contained, in His infinitude, within every finite
object of this universe.

2. Finite objects are not separate or distinct
from *Brahman,* but are *Brahman* transformed.

Though *Brahman* transformed is the universe, He, the source, remains unaffected. So, again, *Brahman* includes all within Himself and also transcends all. " All existence in the Self and the Self in all existence "—is the purport of these passages.

Coming now to *Nishprapancha,* the acosmic ideal, its principal teachings can be illustrated by referring again to the dialogue between Yajnavalkya and Maitreyi. In the course of his teaching, Yajnavalkya says : " Maitreyi, I have said nothing that should frighten or puzzle you. This is the truth that has to be realized. When there is duality, as it were, one sees the other, one hears the other, one touches the other, one knows the other, one welcomes the other. But when the whole is recognized as this Self, who is to be seen by whom, who is to be known by whom ? That Self is to be described only as ' Not this ', ' Not that '. He is incomprehensible, for He cannot be comprehended. He is imperishable, unattached, unfettered."

Other passages in the *Upanishads* employ the figure of clay and its various modifications. " In words or speech alone the modification originates and exists. In reality there is no such thing as modification. It is merely a name, and the clay alone is real." So the universe of name and form is in name and form alone. For *Brahman* is the only reality. On this point the *Mundaka Upanishad* says thus : " He who has attained the highest knowledge becomes one with the Universal Self, freed from

Namarupa—name and form—as the flowing streams enter into, and become united with, the sea, leaving name and form behind."

Samkara founded his philosophy of non-dualism and the doctrine of *Maya* upon these teachings of the *Upanishads*. The world, he declares, is a misreading of God. The finite is a misinterpretation of the Infinite. Samkara, however, nowhere asserts that the world of plurality is non-existent as some of his Western interpreters declare. According to him, the world ' is ' and ' is not '. As he says, it is not non-existent 'like the son of a barren woman '. It is real as long as we experience it in relative consciousness ; the while it is experienced, it possesses an empirical reality. It is unreal only when obliterated in the absolute consciousness.

What then is the underlying truth of the relation between the world of finite objects and *Brahman* as revealed in the *Upanishads* ? Two doctrines seem to prevail among the philosophers of India— *Parinamavada* or the doctrine of transformation as propounded by Ramanuja, and *Vivartavada* or the doctrine of superimposition and the theory of *Maya* as held by Samkara. In the one the universe is an emanation from *Brahman,* and in that sense all is *Brahman*. In the other, the universe of appearance is superimposed upon *Brahman*. As we see the snake on the rope, so do we see the universe on *Brahman*. The reality is *Brahman*—the One without a second.

These two interpretations of reality have been variously understood by Western scholars, who have often identified them with pantheism and illusionism respectively.

We have already noted that the theory of *Maya* is not illusionism ; for the world of phenomena possesses an empirical reality, though not an absolute one, and is therefore neither false nor absolutely real. It has a kind of intermediate existence—it ' is ' and ' is not '.

Is then the theory of emanation identical with pantheism ? Pantheism may be defined as the identification of God with Nature. The sum-total of this universe is, according to it, identical with God. Nowhere in the *Upanishads* is to be found such an identification. It is said that God has become transformed as this universe, and yet He remains the same as before, for He is not only immanent but also transcendent. This transcendental aspect of God is emphasized again and again nearly everywhere in the *Upanishads*. This interpretation can in no respect be regarded as pantheism.

Furthermore, when it is declared that all is *Brahman,* this ' all ' is not what we sense or perceive. The universe is in reality an emanation from Him, and He is the indwelling Spirit in every object of the universe. We can comprehend this truth about the emanation and the indwelling of Spirit only after gaining what is known as the mystic experience or intuition of *Brahman*.

Which of these two doctrines then is the actual teaching of the *Upanishads*? The answer to this question is that they favour neither the one nor the other of these apparently antagonistic interpretations of Reality, though both of these can be deduced from them. The truth is that these *Vedic* scriptures did not in any sense attempt to propound a set of systematic doctrines. The sages were entirely satisfied with their mystic experiences and accorded simple utterance to what was revealed to them while they were in that state. And these mystic experiences, if compared, will reveal rather harmony than discord. In these revelations we find a philosophy and process of experience rather than a philosophy of doctrines. And as we analyse this process, we find that the primary step in the search for reality is the negation or denial of all external objects of experience. The *Atman* is neither ' this ' nor ' that '—*Neti Neti Atma*. As the sages became deeply absorbed in meditation, as they rose above physical perception, above the subtle and casual ' sheaths ', this universe of finite objects and the universe of ideas were obliterated from their consciousness, and there remained the One Existence without a second. " Who is there to see whom ? Who is there to know whom ? " " The knower of *Brahman* becomes verily *Brahman*." Time, space and causation, which are the conditions of experiencing the objective universe, cease to exist when one is in that state.

On return from this unitary consciousness, a mystic, illumined in regard to the nature of the abiding reality, may be either in the normal state of consciousness, or in *Bhavamukha*—an intermediate state in which he has the empirical as well as the transcendental consciousness.

In the normal state he perceives finite objects, and is aware that this finitude is a misreading of the Infinite. Behind every finite object lies the Infinite, the indwelling Spirit. Sri Ramakrishna illustrates this state by the example of a man who has seen that inside all pillows is cotton. He does not actually see the cotton afterwards, but rather sees the pillow cases, and yet he knows that cotton is inside the cases of pillows of all forms and sizes.

In *Bhavamukha,* the intermediate state, the mystic may have an empirical consciousness of the objective universe, but he is also aware of the *Ananda,* the blissful *Brahman* vibrating in all. To illustrate this also Sri Ramakrishna makes use of an analogy, this time of wax dolls. The dolls may be of various forms and sizes, but one sees the wax assuming these forms and sizes. Thus does the mystic see *Brahman* assuming many forms and names. But he sees with never-failing vision that all is *Brahman.*

Both these doctrines, then, find their authority and truth in the *Upanishads,* yet neither in itself gives the whole truth about reality.

VI

Concerning types of knowledge, the *Mundaka Upanishad* speaks in specific terms :
Theory of Knowledge.
" There are two kinds of knowledge—the lower or *Apara,* and the higher or *Para.* Intellectual understanding of the scriptures, phonetics, the code of rituals, grammar, etymology, prosody and astronomy, and the different branches of science and art, form the lower knowledge. The higher knowledge is that by which is realized and attained the imperishable Truth."

The lower knowledge, being of the intellect and the senses, is limited to the objective world of experience. Empirical knowledge is concerned with the finite alone. *Brahman* or *Atman,* which is ' unseen but seeing, unheard but hearing, unperceived but perceiving, unknown but knowing ', cannot be made the object of empirical knowledge. And yet the culmination of wisdom is the knowledge of *Brahman.* In the *Chandogya Upanishad* we read of Uddalaka enquiring of his son Svetaketu, " Have you inquired about that knowledge by which we hear the unheard, by which we perceive the unperceived, by which we know the unknown ? "

The intellect cannot grasp this knowledge, and reason inevitably brings us to the conclusion that *Brahman* or *Atman* is unknown and unknowable. " Not by study, not by intellect, not by erudition is the *Atman* attained," declares the *Katha Upanishad*. And the *Taittiriya Upanishad* describes the *Atman* as "That from which speech along with the mind turns away not able to apprehend."

This *Para-vidya* or the higher knowledge, which reveals to us the unknown, is neither an objective knowledge nor a subjective experience in the sense of mental cognition or feeling as understood in the West; it is rather 'being' and 'becoming'. "A knower of *Brahman* becomes verily *Brahman*." Metaphysically, it is the *Nirvikalpa* knowledge in which the three categories of empirical knowledge—the knower, the object of knowledge and the process of knowledge—are transcended. It is identical with *Turiya* or consciousness in its pristine, transcendental condition. But it is to be distinguished specially from the degeneration of consciousness into a condition of blankness; for it is a state of illumination. The following description of the transcendental state makes this point clear : "This indescribable, ineffable, supreme joy is perceived as—This is That. How can I express That? Is That a borrowed light, or does It shine by Itself? There the sun does not shine, nor the moon, nor the stars, nor lightning, nor fire. That shining, every other object shines. It is the light of That that gives light unto all." By the practice of *Yoga* or spiritual disciplines man attains to this state of transcendental consciousness and realises the identity of his inner Self with the Divine.

The knowledge of the Self is the highest purpose of man, the supreme goal of his life. " Blessed is he who attains to this supreme wisdom in this very life ; if he does not, his life is in vain." All beings in the universe, it is asserted everywhere in the *Upanishads,* are moving towards this end—the realization of the Infinite Self. For, the Infinite, the *Sat-chid-ananda* (the Absolute Existence, the Absolute Knowledge and the Absolute Bliss), is the indwelling Self in all. And in all men is the impulse to express and to unfold and realize one's own being. Behind the struggles of life is this urge to know the Self. Even when one struggles blindly for life, to find love and happiness, and to gather knowledge, one is in reality moved by that urge.

The nature of the Self is *Sat* or Existence, *Chit* or Knowledge, and *Ananda* or Bliss and Love. Some philosophers of the West, having caught a glimpse of the true Self of man, have concluded that we realize the ideal of life by perfectly expressing the infinite through the finite. So in the West there is a universal tendency to find and express God in the finite universe,—to revel in a creative appreciation of His joy through the body, the senses, the mind and all external material forms. This romantic ideal would, no doubt, be pleasing and comforting to those who know of no other bliss.

But such a realization of life has all the limitations of a purely sensational and sense-bound philosophy ; it offers nothing to heal the sores and sufferings of the inner man. It is, in effect, an effort to idealize the real, to compromise our weaknesses and our failures, and not an attempt to realize the real nature of the Self. The sages of the *Upanishads*, on the other hand, point out that man is in reality the Infinite Self, and that his attempt to express his real nature through the finite is necessarily a misdirected effort prompted by ignorance. For the Infinite, declare these sages, can never be expressed through the finite, and the aim of all the struggles of life is to learn just this.

The vanity of earthly life is brought home to the mind of man when the experience of repeated failures teaches him that within the limits of life itself no solution of its riddle can be discovered, and that it is folly to hope for infinite happiness, infinite knowledge and immortality in the life of the body and the senses. It is then that he turns to the Source of all light, happiness, and existence—his own true Self. And by knowing the Self through the process of ' being ' and ' becoming ' It, he attains the supreme goal of life. For he realizes the transcendental Self which is *Sat,* Existence ; *Chit,* Knowledge ; and *Ananda,* Bliss or Love.

This in brief is the teaching of the *Upanishads* with reference to what we might realize upon this earth and in this life.

VII

In all beings exists the Self. " In the heart of all—whatever there is in the universe—abides the Lord," declares the *Isa Upanishad*. He who has attained the highest wisdom by rising above the differences which exist in the sphere of name and form, perceives only sameness where another would perceive infinite diversity. From the absolute point of view, no difference exists in beings and things ; but empirically, with reference to this world, there is difference and diversity between one individual and another. But this empirical difference is not, however, one of kind but only one of degree in which the *Atman* is manifested. In fact beings are higher or lower according to the degree of manifestation of the higher reality. The Self exists equally in all, but all do not exist equally in It, since It is not revealed equally to all. Here in the teachings of the *Upanishads* is suggested a process of evolution not of the Self but of the forms of life as they increasingly reveal the nature and the power of the Self.

This idea is made clear in the following passage of the *Aitareya Aranyaka* : " He who knows the gradual unfoldment of the Self in him, obtains for himself a greater development. There are herbs and trees and animals, and he knows the Self gradually unfolding in them. For in herbs and trees sap only is seen, but in animals there is thought. Among animals, again, the Self develops gradually, for in some sap is seen as well as thought, but in others thought is absent. And in man, again, the Self reveals itself gradually, for he is most endowed with self-consciousness. He says what he has known, he sees what he has known, he knows what is to happen tomorrow, he knows the gross and the subtle. Through the mortal he desires the immortal—thus is he endowed. In other animals, only hunger and thirst are a kind of understanding. But they do not say what they have known, nor do they see what they have known. They do not know what is to happen tomorrow, nor do they know the gross and the subtle. They go so far and no further."

We see that, though the *Atman* exists in all beings, there is a larger degree of manifestation of It in some of them than in others. The *Atman* or the real Self, when It is identifying Itself with individual mind, body and senses, is cognized as the *Jiva,* individual being. It then diversifies Itself into plant life, animal life and human life, just as, to quote the favourite illustration in the *Vedanta* literature, universal space is cut off into the shape of a room, a jar and other similar objects. The *Chit* or Pure Consciousness is not the limited self we know of, neither is It the same as reason or instinct. When It is reflected through the mind and the senses, we call it reason, instinct and perception. But these are degenerations of this Pure Consciousness, the *Chit.*

In lower animals it is called merely instinct ; in man it is reason and self-consciousness. When this self-consciousness reaches the higher stages of its evolution, man feels the summons of the Infinite Self, and starts on the path of realization of the Divine.

Sat-chit-ananda—absolute existence, absolute knowledge and absolute blessedness—are not qualities of the Self but are its essence ; that is to say, there is no distinction between them and the Self Itself. The three are one ; only we perceive the one thing in three different aspects. That eternal consciousness of the Self reflecting through the mind of man becomes reason and instinct. Its differences are all due to differences in the mediums through which it is revealed. As the heart becomes purer, it becomes a better reflector of the *Atman.* It is only in the *Turiya,* the transcendental state, that Consciousness is revealed in Its purity as absolute existence, absolute knowledge and absolute bliss. Hence the *Taittiriya Upanishad* describes it as *Pranaramam,* sportiveness of cosmic life ; *Mana-anandam,* the delight of the mind ; and *Santi-sam-riddham amritam,* highest peace and immortality.

VIII

The term *Moksha* implies freedom from all

Moksha or Freedom, and Immortality.

limitations, bondages and imperfections, as well as release from birth and death. It is the state of oneness with God, and is the birthright of every

6

man. The soul in its real nature is, as we have
seen, free and divine, and for man freedom comes
with this knowledge of his true Self. Submerged
in ignorance, man considers himself finite, bound
and miserable. So bondage lies in ignorance, and
freedom in dissipating it by the knowledge of the
Self and in realizing one's true nature. *Moksha* is
just this recognition of one's divine Self, and not a
transformation into something else. It is the
discovery of the truth that has always been.

The *Chandogya Upanishad* brings out this fact
as follows : " As people ignorant of the presence of
a golden treasure, which has been hidden under-
ground, may walk over it again and again and yet
never find it, so all beings, though every moment
living in *Brahman,* never find Him, for he is
hidden by a covering of ignorance." Again
the same *Upanishad* says : " *Brahman* is the Self
within, untouched by any deed, ageless and
deathless, free from grief, free from hunger and
thirst. The etheric centre within the heart, where
dwells *Brahman,* is like a boundary which separates
That from the mundane world. The day and the
night do not cross that boundary, nor old age, nor
death ; neither grief, nor pleasure, nor good, nor
evil deeds reach That. All evil shuns That,
because That is free and can never be touched
by any impurity."

Thus, despite our ignorance, the pure, perfect,
divine nature of the *Atman* remains quite unaffected.

Similarly, Christ has said, " The light shineth in darkness and the darkness comprehendeth it not " ; " Know ye the truth, and the truth shall make you free " ; and " The Kingdom of God is at hand, watch and pray."

One Indian philosopher has defined *Moksha* as *Svarajyasiddhi* or the attainment of one's own kingdom. The exact nature of this state of liberation cannot be defined in rational terms, for it is identical with the supra-rational *Turiya* or transcendental consciousness. But that it is not a negative state of existence is certain. It is always described as infinite and ineffable joy of a positive type, realizable, yet not to be expressed. To define is to limit, but this state is illimitable, infinite.

In the *Upanishads* the state of *Moksha* or liberation is described as realization of our oneness with *Brahman*. In the words of the *Mundaka Upanishad,* " As the flowing rivers enter into the sea, losing their names and forms, even so the wise man, freed from name and form, attains the supreme Divine Being. Verily, he who knows *Brahman* becomes *Brahman*. No one ignorant of *Brahman* is ever born in his family. Such a knower of *Brahman* overcomes evil. He passes beyond all sorrow. Freed from the fetters of the heart, he becomes immortal."

The *Upanishads* do not recognize the absolute reality of the individual self. The individuality which we so fondly cling to in this life, and hope to retain through eternity, is in reality derived from our identification, through ignorance, of the *Atman*—the eternal Subject—with the non-self. When the Self identifies itself with body, mind or senses, it appears as an individual being. In common experience too we discern that. Though we are clinging to our individual bodies, we are losing them from moment to moment in the process of change that is continually at work. The *Atman,* which is changeless, is the real man. Our true individuality lies in It, and in It alone we find the fullest expression of our being.

Moksha may be attained in this life, or it may be reached after death. Both these forms of liberation are recognized in the *Upanishads*. The first one is called *Jivanmukti* or freedom attained in this life. For the man who has reached Self-knowledge through transcendental consciousness, the vision of the world has changed into the vision of Reality or *Brahman*. He is called the ' living free '. For such a man delusion has vanished for ever. He is free from selfish desires, for the sense of want is annihilated in him once for all by the ineffable experience of Self-realization. His only delight is now in God or the Self, for he is truly conscious of ' living, moving, and having his being in God '. And the transcendental intuition which has brought him the realization of his oneness with God, gives him also the realization of the same God in all beings. His life, therefore, becomes one of service in the light of the knowledge of the one Self and one God in all.

The second form of liberation is called *Videha Mukti,* or freedom after death. In this the man concerned realizes the highest knowledge of the Self and its identity with *Brahman* only at the time of death. This, however, can be achieved only if one has disciplined and prepared oneself all through life, with this as the only aim. Liberation, whether it is gained in life itself or after death, puts an end to re-birth once for all.

Moksha is, therefore, a stopping of the wheel of birth and death, cutting asunder the thread of ignorance by the sword of knowledge. Hence this state is identical with immortality.

The ideal of immortality as taught in the *Upanishads* does not imply a continuous existence of the individual after death but rather the fact that the true Self is unborn and undying. It is said in the *Katha Upanishad* : " The Self, the Knower, is neither born nor dies. This ancient One is unborn, eternal, everlasting. This ancient One is never destroyed even when the body dies. If the slayer thinks he slays, if the slain thinks he is slain, neither of them knows. He slays not, nor is He slain. Subtler than the subtle, greater than the great, this *Atman* dwells in the hearts of all. He who is free from desire and free from grief, with his mind and senses purified, beholds the glory of the Self."

The question is not whether the soul continues its existence after death or not ; for, as it is affirmed by the Upanishads, the Self is neither born, nor does It die. That which has birth must also have death. On this point, Swami Vivekananda says :

" I am studying a book ; page after page is being read and turned over. Who changes ? Who comes and goes ? Not I, but the book. This whole Nature is a book before the soul ; chapter after chapter is being read and turned over, and every now and then a scene opens. That is read and turned over. A fresh one comes but the soul is ever the same— eternal. It is Nature[1] that is changing, not the soul of man. This never changes. Birth and death are in Nature, not in you. Yet the ignorant are deluded. Just as we under delusion think that the sun is moving and not the earth, in exactly the same way we think that we are dying, and not Nature. These are all, therefore, hallucinations, just as it is a hallucination when we think that the fields are moving and not the railway train. Exactly in the same manner is the hallucination of birth and death."

So immortality is not continuity in time, but participation, by knowledge of identity, in the consciousness and entity of the eternal Divine. Through ignorance we identify ourselves with body and

[1] Within the category of Nature is also classified the body, mind, and senses, for these are not the Self.

ego ; through ignorance we think ourselves to be subject to birth and death. With the dawn of knowledge we realize our true Self which is recognized as identical with the Supreme Divinity, and with this realization, we are released from the wheel of birth and death.

But so long as the state of ignorance lasts, and the concomitant identification with the non-self continues, we have to undergo birth and death, that is, we remain subject to the laws of *Karma* and the woes of mortality. This is the doctrine of reincarnation propounded by the *Upanishads*. In the words of the *Chandogya Upanishad,* " Those who depart from this world, without having realized the Self, find no freedom in all the worlds, while those who depart, having realized the Self, find freedom everywhere."

IX

The *Brihadaranyaka Upanishad* furnishes a clear explanation of the problem of death and reincarnation. We read in it : " When the body grows weak either through sickness or old age, the departing soul separates itself from the body as a mango or a fig is separated from its stalk, and hastens to begin another life. When that soul, having sunk into weakness, is about to make its journey to another world, and appears to be no

Karma and Reincarnation.

longer conscious, then it gathers its senses around it and lives for a while within the heart. No more does it see any external form or colour. Then the point of the heart is lighted by the light of the soul, and by that light it departs either through the eye or the skull, or through other apertures of the body. When it thus departs, life departs with it, and when life departs, the rest of the senses and vital spirits also depart. The soul is conscious, and with consciousness it goes to the next world. And the impressions of its knowledge and the deeds of this life follow it. As a caterpillar, having reached the end of a blade of grass, takes hold of another blade of grass and then draws itself together towards it, so does the soul, after having given up this present body, take hold of another body, and draw itself together towards it.

"This Self is indeed *Brahman*. But because of Its association and identification with limiting adjuncts, It appears to consist of intellect, mind, sight, and hearing; of different elements such as earth, water, air, ether, and fire; of desire and no desire; of anger and no anger; of right and wrong; and of all other things. As his deeds and thought in fact are, so does he appear to become. A man of good deeds becomes good; a man of bad deeds, bad. He becomes pure by pure deeds, impure by evil deeds.

"As is a person's desire, so is his will; as is his will, so is his deed; as is his deed, so will he reap.

To whatever object a man's mind is attached, to that he goes with the impressions of his deeds. And after having enjoyed the results of his deeds in the other world, he returns from that world to this world of action. Such is the case with the man who desires and has not yet attained the knowledge of Self."

Our future life is thus guided by our deeds and our desires in the present life. The law of *Karma* essentially means that our actions produce results in two ways—in the first place as effects in the shape of happiness and sorrow we reap, and in the next place as actions producing impressions on our minds, the sum total of which forms our character. And our next life is determined by our character formed in the present. In the words of the *Chandogya Upanishad* : "Those whose conduct has been good will attain good birth ; but those whose conduct is evil will verily attain evil birth."

Two paths there are by which souls travel after death—one known as *Pitriyana* or the path of the Fathers, and the other as *Devayana* or the path of the Gods. He who goes by the path of *Pitriyana,* after enjoying the fruits of his good deeds in the *Lokas* or heavenly regions, returns to earth. These heavenly regions are called *Bhogabhumi* or places in which one enjoys the fruits of one's deeds. This earth is *Karmabhumi* or the region of action where we make our future through our deeds ; and it is also the place where we finally realize our freedom.

We are bound to reincarnate again and again until, through knowledge, we ultimately become free. According to the *Upanishads* no soul will be lost.

He who travels by *Devayana* does not return to this world but gradually attains knowledge and freedom in the *Brahmaloka*. This process is known as *Kramamukti* or gradual liberation. But for him who gains the knowledge of the Self in this very life, freedom from the wheel of birth and death becomes possible in this world itself.[1] In the words of the *Brihadaranyaka Upanishad* : " When all the desires of the heart are destroyed at the dawn of the knowledge of *Brahman,* the mortal becomes immortal ; then man attains *Brahman* even in this life. And as the slough of a snake lies cast away on an ant-hill, so lies the body. The Spirit, disembodied and immortal, becomes united with *Brahman*.

" If a man realizes the Self as one with the blissful *Brahman,* what desire is left to impel him to assume the frailties and weaknesses of the body ? One who realizes the Self residing within this frail body as one with *Brahman,* is verily *Brahman*. All the worlds are within him, and he is in all the worlds. Those who realize this truth of *Brahman* become immortal. Others, ignorant of the glory of this Self, remain within the bonds of birth and death, and verily that is misery.

---

[1] A third path, which leads to the joyless regions of the wicked souls, is also mentioned in the *Upanishads*.

" They who know the Self as the life of life, the eye of the eye, the ear of the ear, the mind of the mind, they indeed know the ancient primeval *Brahman*. By the purified mind alone can this be known. He who sees difference goes from death to death.

" Let a man, after he has heard about this Self, meditate on Him in order to attain wisdom. He must give up all vain talk, for that is particularly fatiguing to the organ of speech.

" This glorious, unborn Self, who is the intelligence of the intellect, who is surrounded by the senses, who is the ruler and lord of all, resides within the sanctuary of the heart. He is not touched by any deed ; neither does He become great by great works, nor belittled by evil works. He is the ruler, the lord, the protector of all. He is like a bridge which crosses the ocean of the miseries of the world.

" The Brahmins, desiring to know Him, study the *Vedas,* offer sacrifices, and practise penance. Knowing Him one becomes a seer. Desiring to know Him alone, they take to the life of renunciation. Desiring Him alone, they give up all other desires."

X

We have learned that the highest freedom is attained through knowledge of the real Self. It is identical with the realization of our oneness with *Brahman,* who, in the words of the *Brihadaranyaka*

Spiritual Disciplines and Ethical Life.

Upanishad, ' is far above hunger and thirst, above sorrow and confusion, above old age and death '. We have also learned that the Self, in Its true nature, is free, divine and pure, and that ignorance only hides this true nature of It. Just so does the Bible also declare, " The Light shineth in darkness ; and the darkness comprehendeth it not." (*Gospel according to St. John.*)

This idea of a Self, pure and undefiled, which is the basis of the teachings in the *Upanishads,* is to be found in every religion. In the *Old Testament,* for example, Adam, the first-born, was pure, but this purity was obliterated by his own evil deeds. And the very essence of Christian teachings is that the lost paradise may be recovered, that one's lost innocence may be regained, that the pristine purity of the soul may return, and that the Kingdom of Heaven lies within. Similarly, the Buddhist conception of *Nirvana* denotes a state beyond the world of relative objects ; and the whole philosophical system of the Buddhists revolves about rediscovering that state of bliss. And so the *Moksha* or liberation of the *Upanishads* is only another instance of the cry of man in his misery for help to find the bliss he has lost and to rid himself of his present state of helplessness and restless striving.

Since the veil of ignorance covers the perfection of the Self, spiritual disciplines are necessary for removing that evil. With their help the light of knowledge begins to shine on the aspirant, and he becomes

' perfect even as our Father in Heaven is perfect '. These disciplines consist in the observance of moral laws and the practice of *Yoga.*

In the West as well as in the East, this teaching is often misunderstood by some. They ask if man is pure and divine by nature, may he not dispense with moral obligations ? In this connection it is interesting to note how Sri Ramakrishna, the holy prophet of Dakshineswar, treated a man who posed as a *Vedantist* and at the same time led a bad life. When advised by the sage to learn self-control before aspiring to be a *Vedantist,* the man replied, " I am divine and pure. My actions do not affect me. There is no evil, for evil is but an illusion." At this, Sri Ramakrishna indignantly remarked, " I despise such teachings. Never support your weakness by quoting the scriptures." The truth of the matter is that, though man is divine, his real nature is hid in ignorance. Perfect observance of moral principles and perfect self-control are the only means by which the veil of ignorance can be removed. Ethical conduct is the very basis of spiritual life, but it is not the whole of religion. The *Upanishads* declare that when the transcendental level of consciousness is reached and man realizes his Divinity, he rises above all laws. " He is not afflicted by the thought, ' Why have I not done what is good, why have I committed sin ? ' The immortal is beyond both, beyond good and evil."

But again we must remember that though he is above all laws, his nature has been so transformed that he has become the very embodiment of goodness. No evil can be done by a man who has had such an experience. Swami Vivekananda has beautifully described the state of such a saint in the following words : " Even if he lives in the body and works incessantly, he works only to do good ; his lips speak only benediction to all ; his hands do only good works ; his mind can think only good thoughts ; his presence is a blessing wherever he goes. He is himself a living blessing. Such a man will, by his very presence, change even the most wicked persons into saints. Can such men do any evil, can they do wicked deeds ? There is, you must remember, all the difference of pole to pole between realization and mere talking."

What then of the charge that the *Upanishads* contain no systematic ethical teachings ? It is urged that, if there is but one existence, and if all beings form one unity, there can be no possibility of relations between men, and as a consequence, moral laws will lose all meaning. But this idea of unity of existence, far from being a weakness, is the only basis upon which true ethical life is possible. If men were really so separated from one another that the gulf between them could not be bridged, the ethical ideal of love would be meaningless. For, if the experience of separate individual selves is an abiding fact, then each man would always live for himself alone, without any regard for the good of others, as he is actually doing now in his state of ignorance. Through the ideal of unity we learn the truth that by loving others we love ourselves, and that by hating others we hate ourselves. "Love thy neighbour as thyself," is a precept we first find in the *Upanishads,* and later echoed by Buddha and re-echoed by Christ. You are asked to love your neighbour as yourself, for verily he is yourself.

Thus morality, which differs in its expression in different countries and among different peoples has this single definition : Whatever leads us towards unity with God and all beings, is good, and whatever draws us away from this ideal of unity is evil.

Though the absolute truth consists in this oneness which we have been discussing, in this world of relativity the ordinary man is far away from the realization of this unity. Ethical laws have thus their value inasmuch as their observance leads us to the perception of the absolute truth of oneness, which is identical with Self-realization.

In this book it has been insisted upon again and again that the divine nature of man is covered by ignorance, and that knowledge alone can reveal it. This knowledge is not essentially an intellectual mastery of some abstruse metaphysical doctrines, but is rather identical with the process of ' being ' and ' becoming '. And the condition of ' being ' and ' becoming ' is the transformation of our whole

nature, which is made possible by ' the renewal of
our minds ', in the words of St. Paul, and by what the
Upanishads denominate as ' self-control ' or check
of selfish desires, passions and impulses. This ideal
of self-control is summed up in the *Katha Upanishad*
as follows : " Know the body to be the chariot, the
intellect the charioteer, the mind the reins, the
Self the lord in the chariot. The senses are the
horses, the objects their road. He who has no
control over his mind and is without discrimination,
permits his senses to become unmanageable like
untamed horses. But he who is discriminative and
whose mind is restrained, controls his senses like
trained horses. The man who has a discriminative
intellect for his charioteer, and a well regulated
mind for the reins, reaches the end of the journey,
the supreme abode of *Vishnu,* the all-pervading One.
This Self, hidden in all beings, reveals not Himself
unto all ; but He is comprehended by the pure ones
of sharpened and purified intellect."

A purified intellect implies essentially inner
purity of both heart and mind, and also the proper
regulation of outer conduct in the light of moral
principles as a means to that end. Certain injunctions concerning the ways of attaining this purity of
heart are scattered throughout these scriptures. In
the *Taittiriya Upanishad* we read : " One should
observe the following : Truthfulness in word, deed
and thought ; self-denial and the practice of
austerity ; self-control and poise ; performance of

the everyday duties of life with a cheerful heart and unattached mind. Above all follow the way of truth—speak the truth. Perform your duties. Deviate not from the path of good. Revere greatness. Do only such actions as are blameless. Always show reverence to those who are superior and great. Give no gifts without love and reverence, but give in plenty with joy, with humility and with compassion. If at any time there is any doubt with regard to right conduct, follow those great souls who are guileless, who are of good judgment and who are devoted to the truth."

Inner purity is achieved by complete self-abnegation, as by it we free ourselves from all selfish and personal desires. Detachment from the lower self or ego, and attachment to the higher Self or love of God, are the fruits of a moral life. Sir S. Radhakrishnan has beautifully expressed this truth in the following words : " If a man's desire is the flesh, he becomes an adulterer ; if things of beauty, an artist ; if God, a saint."

The fact is that until one has conquered his desires, the truth cannot shine in him. The *Katha Upanishad* points out these truths when it says : " The good is one thing, and different indeed is the pleasant. These two, having different ends, engage men differently. It is well for him who chooses the good ; he who chooses the pleasant misses the true goal."

Giving up of fleshly desires means in the end the renunciation of 'me' and 'mine'. Swami Viveka-nanda expresses himself thus on this point : "What is the watchword of all ethical codes? 'Not I but Thou'; and this 'I' is the outcome of the Infinite behind, trying to manifest Itself in the outside world. This little 'I' is the result, and it will have to go back and join the Infinite, its own nature. Every time you say, 'Not I, my brother, but thou', you are trying to go back, and every time you say, 'I and not thou', you take the false step of trying to manifest the Infinite through the sense-world. That brings struggle and evil into the world, but after a time renunciation must come, eternal renunciation. The little 'I' is dead and gone. Why care so much for this little life? All these vain desires of living and enjoying this life, here or in some other place, bring death."

As a parallel to this idea may be mentioned the central teaching of Christ : "For whosoever will save his life shall lose it ; and whosoever will lose his life for my sake shall find it."

XI

For the realization of the truth of God in our own souls, the sages have pres-cribed three steps, namely *Sravana* or hearing, *Manana* or reflection, and *Nidhidhyasana* or meditation. We must first

Spiritual Consciousness.

hear of the truth of God and of the *Atman,* and we must hear this truth from one unto whom it has been revealed. Great stress is laid upon the necessity of seeking a *Guru* or teacher, one who is a living embodiment of the ideal. Samkara has rightly said : " Rare and blessed is the combination of these three—human birth, desire for freedom, and association with a holy man." In all Indian scriptures an aspirant after spiritual enlightenment is strongly advised to associate himself with a holy man and to revere him. In the *Katha Upanishad* we read : " Wonderful must be the teacher and wonderful must be the pupil." " He that hath a teacher alone knows," declares the *Chandogya Upanishad.*

But hearing is not enough. No true teacher demands a blind acceptance of his teaching. We must reflect in order to gain intellectual conviction of what we learn. The study of logic or of science aids us in reflection, and independent philosophical thinking trains the mind. But this mental training must be finally supplemented by meditation.

Our imperfections are caused by ignorance, and right knowledge alone can dissipate or destroy this ignorance. These imperfections are immediate experiences, and they cannot therefore be removed by mere intellectual awareness of the true Self ; another immediate experience is required to destroy the present relative experience of imperfection. And that is the real meaning of describing religion

as realization or experience. The surest means
towards this realization or immediate perception
of the truth of the Self and God is the habit of
meditation.

The highest form of this meditation as stated in
the *Upanishads* is concentration upon the truth
' *Aham Brahmasmi* '—' I am *Brahman* '. This is the
Absolute *Brahman* which is one with our inner
Self—a truth that has been stated and restated in these
pages. But the exact nature of the special form
of meditation cannot be understood unless it is
learned under a competent teacher. In the *Upanishads* we discover only hints regarding the various
methods of meditation. Hence the exact method
can be learned only through the right kind of
instruction. From the *Guru,* then, we must first
hear and learn to reflect and meditate, for without
him we remain in ignorance.

In these scattered hints upon the subject of meditation, the Upanishads point to the heart of man as
the inner sanctuary where dwells the Supreme
Brahman. That is the central truth of the whole
body of these scriptures. As aids to meditation, the
Upanishads have accepted various objects as
symbols of *Brahman,* and of these the mystic
syllable ' Om ' is the most important. The following
passage from the *Mundaka Upanishad* brings out
the importance of this syllable : " Having taken
what is taught in the *Upanishads* as the bow, affix
to it the arrow sharpened by devotional worship.

Then, with a concentrated heart, draw it and hit the mark—that imperishable *Brahman*. *Om* is the bow, the arrow the individual soul, and *Brahman* the target. With a tranquil heart, take aim. Become absorbed in Him even as the arrow becomes one with the target. In Him are woven the heaven, the earth, the sky, the mind, and the *Prana*. Know that one Self alone. Give up all vain talk. He is the bridge to immortality. He lives there within the heart where all the nerves meet like the spokes of a wheel in the nave. Meditate on the Self as *Om*."

XII

The high literary quality and the poetic beauty of
The Literary Perfection of the Upanishads.
these ancient Indian scriptures cannot adequately be conveyed to a reader unacquainted with Sanskrit, an ancient and obsolete language difficult to learn. Perhaps a quotation from Swami Vivekananda, himself a saint of modern India and a learned exponent of Hindu religious thought, may give one an indication of their merit as literature. Says the Swami :

" Apart from their merit as the greatest philosophy, from their merit as theology, from their success in showing the path of salvation to mankind, the *Upanishadic* literature is the most sublime in the world. Here is shown in full force the introspective and intuitive Hindu mind. There are poems of sublimity in all nations, but you will find that almost without exception, their ideal is to grasp the sublime in the material. Take for instance, Milton, Dante, Homer, or any of the Western poets. There are passages in them which express the sublime wonderfully; but there is always the endeavour to grasp it through the senses and the muscles, infinitely expanding them, as it were, in the infinity of space. We find the same attempt in the *Samhita* portion of the *Vedas*. But there they soon found out that the infinite could not be reached in that way, that even infinite space and expansion and infinite external Nature could not express the ideas that were struggling to find expression in their minds; and they fell back upon other explanations. Henceforth the language became new, as it were, in the *Upanishads*; it became almost negative; it appears almost chaotic at times—taking you beyond the senses, sometimes going half way towards the goal, as it were, and leaving you there pointing out to you something which you cannot sense, but which at the same time you feel certain is there. The language and the thought of the *Upanishads* fall upon you like the blade of a sword, like a blow from a hammer, and appeal directly to your heart. And there is no mistaking the meaning. Every tone of that music is true and produces its full effect. If this be human literature, it cannot but be the production of a race still in possession of its national vigour."

CHAPTER IV

THE MESSAGE OF THE BHAGAVAD GITA

I

EMBEDDED in one Book of the great Indian epic,
the *Mahabharata,* occurs the
Bhagavad Gita or the Song Celestial, the most popular of all the
religious literature of India. The date of this great
document is assigned by scholars to a time some-
where between the fifth and the second centuries
before Christ. Its influence upon the minds of
prophets, reformers, and ascetics, and upon the
laity—indeed upon the whole of Hindu life and
thought through countless generations—is recognis-
ed by all students of Indian culture. Without fear
of contradiction it may be said to be the Holy Bible
of India, though, unlike the *Upanishads,* it is not
regarded as *Sruti* or revealed scripture, but only as
Smriti or tradition elaborating the doctrines of the
Upanishads.[1]

Introduction :
1. The Teacher
and the Disciple.

---

[1] The *Sruti* or revealed scripture is regarded as having
originated from God Himself. The *Smriti* embodies the
teachings of Divine Incarnations, prophets, saints and sages.
It derives its authority from the *Sruti,* which it must in
no way contradict. The distinction emphasised in this is

The following invocation on the *Gita* gives expression to what has just now been said : " All the *Upanishads* are the cows, the son of the cowherd (Krishna) is the milker, Partha (Arjuna) is the calf, men of purified intellect are the drinkers, and the supreme nectar known as the *Gita* is the milk."

The song Celestial is written in the form of a dialogue between Krishna, who may be called the Christ of India, and his friend and disciple, Arjuna. This Krishna is the Divine One, the ' Lord who abides within the heart of all beings '. It is a conception which expresses the basic truth in all Indian religious thought, namely, that all existence is a manifestation of God, and that God exists in all beings as the innermost Self. In every heart is Krishna concealed, and when the veil of ignorance which covers the inner sanctuary is withdrawn, we hear the voice of Krishna, the very voice of God. In the *Gita,* Krishna openly declares himself to be one with *Brahman,* the Infinite Self, and urges Arjuna to attain to ' My being '. " Freed from attachment, fear and anger," he says, " absorbed in Me, taking refuge in Me, purified by the fire of knowledge, many have attained My being " (IV, 10).

Thus the teacher of the Gita as a historical personage has but a secondary importance. Therein he differs from the Christ of the New Testament, at least the Christ upon whose personality is based

that between revealed scripture on the one hand, and religious commentary and tradition on the other.

the whole religion of Christianity. The *Gita* is mainly concerned with Krishna [1] the teacher, who is identical with the Divine Self or the Infinite in man. Indeed, to those who seek spiritual illumination, it matters little, in the case of both Krishna and Christ, whether these two figures ever existed as historical personages, so long as it is possible for them to attain their heart's desire, namely, union with God—the Universal Self—through the inner Krishna or the living Christ.

And in the *Gita* we find stress laid not on Krishna as an individual personality, but on Krishna in his transcendental aspect, as the Soul of all souls, the great ' I AM '. Arjuna's vision of the Universal

---

[1] " The historical Krishna, no doubt, existed. We meet the name first in the *Chandogya Upanishad* where all we can gather about him is that he was well known in spiritual tradition as a knower of *Brahman,* so well known indeed in his personality and the circumstances of his life, that it was sufficient to refer to him by the name of his mother, as Krishna, son of Devaki, for all to understand who was meant. In the same *Upanishad* we find mention of King Dhritarashtra, son of Vichitravirya, and since tradition associated the two together so closely that they are both of them leading personages in the action of the Mahabharata, we may fairly conclude that they were actually contemporaries, and that the epic is to a great extent dealing with historical characters and in the war of Kurukshetra, with a historical occurrence imprinted firmly on the memory of the race. . . . There is a hint also in the poem of the story or legend of the Avatar's early life in Vrindavan which, as developed by the Puranas into an intense and powerful spiritual symbol, has exercised so profound an influence on the religious mind of India. We have also in the *Harivamsa* an account of Krishna very evidently full of legends, which perhaps formed the basis of the Puranic accounts."—*Essays on the Gita,* by Sri Aurobindo Ghosh.

Form in the body of Krishna, described in the eleventh Chapter of the *Gita*, illustrates this truth

Arjuna, the disciple and friend of whom Krishna is the constant companion, is typically human, being neither a saint nor a sinner, but a struggling human soul seeking to escape from the griefs and miseries of this world. He is represented in the *Gita* as a man of action, a fighter,—a man living in the world, but one confused as to his duty and the true meaning and goal of life, and yet eager to find a way towards peace and freedom.

The *Gita* is therefore in the form of a conversation between Krishna, who is Narayana or God, and Arjuna, who represents *Nara* or man. The *Gita* is the song of God chanted in thrilling notes to the ear of man.

The commentaries upon the *Gita* are numerous ; for each school of philosophy in India has found in it the source of its own metaphysical system, and every philosopher or saint has drawn inspiration from the same fountain-head. So the *Gita* contains the germs of all forms and systems of religious thought, but it cannot itself be limited to any particular system of metaphysics or religion. For it is not a metaphysical treatise, nor is it the fruit of the traditional religious thinking of any particular sect ; rather, one should say, it contains metaphysical truths in their diverse aspects, and embodies every form of religious

2. The Teachings of the Gita.

THE MESSAGE OF THE BHAGAVAD GITA 107

thought, practice and discipline. Conflicting ideas apparently lie side by side unreconciled. A person who holds to one religion as exclusively true will find in the *Gita,* as some Western critics hold, ' different streams of tradition becoming confused in the mind of the author '.

The spirit of catholicity is a prominent feature of all Indian teachings. They evince a spirit of harmony rather than of conflict, of synthesis and toleration rather than of opposition and sectarianism. Infinite is God, infinite are His aspects, and infinite are the ways to reach Him. In the *Rig Veda* we read : " *Ekam sat vipra bahudha vadanti.*"—" Truth is one, sages call it by various names." This ideal of harmony has held its own in India down to the present time. The *Gita* carries this ideal of harmony and universality to its logical conclusion in the process of blending, synthesising, and harmonising conflicting metaphysical ideals and conceptions of spiritual disciplines. " In whatever way men worship me," we read in its pages, " in the same way do I fulfil their desires. It is My path that men tread in all ways " (IV, 11). Sri Aurobindo Ghosh has rightly remarked : " The *Gita* is not a weapon for dialectical warfare ; it is a gate opening on the whole world of spiritual truth and experience, and the view it gives us embraces all the provinces of that supreme region. It maps out, but it does not cut up or build walls or hedges to confine our vision."

Fundamentally the *Gita* insists upon knowledge of Self or God as the only goal of life. All religions, all doctrines spring from God,—and yet no single religion or doctrine can be identified with Him, and none of them possesses any value until we have attained unto Him. All the conflicts of doctrines cease only when He shines in our hearts. " To the knower of *Brahman* who has attained the truth," declares the *Gita,* " all the Vedas are of so much use as a reservoir is when there is a flood everywhere " (II, 46).

In his last utterance, Sri Krishna, the divine teacher, clearly and definitely states the ' supreme word' of the poem, the highest note of the divine discourse : " Hear thou again My supreme word, the profoundest of all. Give thy heart to Me. Be devoted to Me. Sacrifice to Me. Prostrate thyself before Me. Verily shalt thou attain Me. I promise true, for thou art dear to Me. Let go all the formalities of religion and duty ; take refuge in Me alone. I will liberate thee from all thy impurities. Do not grieve " (XVIII, 64-66).

This ' supreme word ' of the *Gita,* though a simple utterance of the profoundest truth, is not easy to follow and realize. Self-surrender, knowingly ' to live, move, and have our being in God ', is central in all religious teachings, or *Yogas,* as they are called in the *Gita.*

These *Yogas* or ways of spiritual attainment, which are peculiar to Indian life, are fully expounded

in the *Gita*. The word Yoga literally means union
—union with God. Its secondary meaning, ' the
path of union with Godhead ', defines the different
Yogas. These paths of attainment may be found
in the earliest Indian scriptures, and they were
known to the sages and adepts of the land. They
are principally four : *Jnana Yoga* or the path of
union through knowledge ; *Raja Yoga* or the path
of realization through meditation and psychic control ; *Bhakti Yoga* or the path of at-one-ment
through love and devotion ; and *Karma Yoga* or the
path of union through work. All of these have not
only been expounded in the *Gita* as the various
methods of attaining union with God, but in its
teachings they stand reconciled, blended, and
harmonized.

Most commentators, however, stress one or
another *Yoga* as the actual teaching of Sri Krishna.
Formerly, either *Jnana Yoga* or *Bhakti Yoga*—
attainment by means of knowledge or devotion—was
stressed ; today much emphasis is put on *Karma
Yoga* or the path of work, as the primary teaching
of the *Gita*. But the fact is that whenever Sri
Krishna speaks of one of them, he naturally puts
extreme i mportance upon that particular one : so
much so each of the *Yogas* in turn assumes the same
importance as the others. The perfect man of the
Gita, with some resemblance to the Aristotelian
conception of the ideal man as the harmonious
embodiment of all the virtues, is one who is active

as well as meditative, who is devotional and at the same time possesses the knowledge of the Self.

The *Gita* is divided into eighteen chapters, which can again be classified into three sections, each comprising six chapters. The first of these three divisions deal with *Karma Yoga,* the path of work, and here the insistence is upon action. The second book is devoted to an exposition of *Jnana Yoga,* the path of knowledge, and here the insistence is upon knowledge of the Self. In this section the subject of *Karma* is not entirely dismissed, but is harmonized with the path of knowledge. The last of these books discusses *Bhakti Yoga,* or the path of love and devotion, and the insistence here is on worship and love of the one Supreme Lord. Here again *Jnana* (knowledge) and *Karma* (work) do not disappear from the book, but are both harmonized with devotion. As Sri Aurobindo Ghosh has beautifully expressed it, " The double path (*Jnana* and *Karma*) becomes the triune way of knowledge, works, and devotion. And the fruit of the sacrifice, the one fruit still placed before the seeker, is attained— union with the Divine Being and oneness with the supreme divine nature." And in and through this triune way of knowledge, works and devotion, runs the thread of *Raja Yoga* or the path of meditation, which insists on poise, self-control, tranquillity and meditative life.

From another angle, the first book, comprising the first six chapters, deals with the true nature of

' *Tvam* ' or ' Thou ' (*i.e.,* the nature of the true Self) occurring in the great *Vedantic* saying, ' *Tat tvamasi* '—' Thou art That '. The second book explains the nature of ' *Tat* ' or ' That ' ; and the last book brings out the truth of the identity of ' Thou ' with ' That '. Thus the great *Vedantic* truth embodied in the saying ' Thou art That ', forms the subject-matter of the *Gita,* and the whole of that scripture is only an exposition of this teaching.

Once, when Sri Ramakrishna was asked, " What does the *Gita* teach ? " he replied,

3. Renunciation is the Central Teaching of the Gita.

" if you utter the word ' *Gita* ', ' *Gita* ', a few times, you begin to say, ' *Tagi* ', ' *Tagi* '—one who has renounced. In other words, the ideal of renunciation is the spirit of the teachings of the *Gita.*"

Renunciation is indeed the beginning, the middle and the end of spiritual life. This spirit of passionless renunciation is inseparable from any of the *Yogas* taught in the *Gita.* Renunciation does not, however, necessarily imply the adoption of monastic life. For it is a discipline that has to be practised by all, whether one be a monk or a man of the world discharging one's respective duties. ' Otherworldliness ', in spite of the associations of the world, does not imply escape into the forest, shunning the duties of everyday life in society. Throughout, the *Gita* insists on the performance of the duties of life with a heart free from attachment and thoughts of worldly gain, and devoted entirely to the adoration of God. It condemns in unmistakable terms the acceptance of monastic life if the spirit of renunciation is lacking in the heart, removing thereby the misconception that the ideal of renunciation can be practised only away from society in a lonely cave or within the walls of a monastery.

The failure to grasp the true spiritual outlook of the *Gita* has led many in modern times to read the ideals of modern secularism into the pages of this ancient Indian scripture. Instead of the ideal of renunciation—the denial of ' me ' and ' mine ' and the conversion of the lusts of the flesh into a passionate love of God—they find in it only a condemnation of ' otherworldliness ' and an insistence on living in the world for the performance of the world's works. The ideal of knowledge, devotion, meditation, and non-attachment, they aver, are subservient to *Karma,* the central doctrine of the *Gita* according to them. So the Western ideals of humanitarian service and social uplift, besides political activity and family life, have been identified with the *Karma Yoga* of the *Gita.* All of these objectives and ideals are of course laudable, and the *Gita* does not condemn them, but it is also certain that it does not teach them as *Karma Yoga.* Granting that these ideals are recognized in the *Gita,* unless they themselves are spiritualized, they have no relation to *Karma Yoga.* Not *Karma,* mere action, but *Karma Yoga,* union with God through action, is the essence of the teaching of the *Gita* on this score.

Thus, not sacrifice for humanity, but service to humanity as a sacrifice unto God, whose image we learn to see in man, is the true ideal. No political activities undertaken with a selfish motive, but duties performed as worship of God ; not merely family life and the performance of the ordinary domestic duties, but a life of non-attachment in the midst of these duties, combined with the knowledge of the nature of one's immutable, eternal Self,—this is the real message of the *Bhagavad Gita*. It is only as these worldly affairs are spiritualized and transformed that they become a part of *Karma Yoga* as expounded in the *Gita*. In short, temporal life and spiritual values stand in a relation of harmony—one divine life, as the *Gita* tells us. Insistence on the performance of *Svadharma* or one's own duty, in the spirit of *Yoga,* is indeed often met with but this insistence loses much of its force with the growth of higher knowledge. Sri Aurobindo has made this issue abundantly clear when he says :

" An inner situation may even arise, as with the Buddha, in which all duties have to be abandoned, trampled on, flung aside in order to follow the call of the Divine within. I cannot think that the *Gita* would solve such an inner situation by sending Buddha back to his wife and father and the government of the Sakya State, or would direct a Ramakrishna to become a *Pundit* in a vernacular school and disinterestedly teach little boys their lessons, or bind down a Vivekananda to support his family and

8

for that to follow dispassionately law or medicine or journalism. The *Gita* does not teach the disinterested performance of duties, but the following of the divine life, the abandonment of all *Dharmas, Sarva-dharman,* to take refuge in the Supreme alone, and the divine activity of a Buddha or a Ramakrishna or a Vivekananda is perfectly in consonance with this teaching."

II

The great poem opens with a description of two armies arrayed against each other, ready for battle. The scene is laid in the field of Kurukshetra where, accompanied by his divine charioteer Krishna, stands Arjuna, the hero, about to give battle to the host of the *Kauravas.* As Arjuna views both the armies he is filled with melancholy. The horrors of war and the terror of death overwhelm him. And he turns to Krishna, who urges him to carry on the fight against his enemies, the enemies of righteousness and truth. Arjuna's feeling of revulsion against useless slaughter meets with Krishna's stern rebuke ; it is, in his words, ' disgraceful and contrary to the attainment of heaven ' (II, 2).

The Battlefield of Kurukshetra.

So, at the very commencement of the great book, we are astonished to see one of the supreme teachers of the spiritual gospel supporting war. What is the explanation of this ?

As we proceed, we discover that the way of realizing the divine consciousness and attaining eternal life and infinite peace, is through complete detachment and self-surrender. We can understand the *Gita* as a holy scripture and Krishna as a divine teacher only when we consider that this war is but an occasion for bringing spiritual truths to our attention. But it is still difficult to understand how the actual war and Krishna's urging to wage it to the end, can be reconciled with any spiritual teaching. The *Gita's* ideal man is certainly not the superman of Nitzsche's imagination, who would crush all opposition in his struggle for power. Quite to the contrary, it is he ' who delights in God ' as a *Yogi,* whose spiritual practices correspond to the life of contemplation which Aristotle considers as the highest attainment of man. And *Yoga* has been defined in the *Gita* as follows : " When the mind, absolutely restrained by the practice of concentration, attains quietude ; when seeing the Self by the self, one is satisfied in one's own Self ; when one feels that infinite bliss which is perceived by the purified intellect and which transcends the senses, and wherein established one never departs from one's real state ; when one regards no other acquisition superior to that ; and when one is not moved even by heavy sorrow,—then let that be known as the state called by the name of *Yoga,* a state of severance from the contact of pain " (VI, 20-23).

But we are still facing the problem of war and the destruction it involves. This Gordian knot of war can easily be cut if we read a symbolic meaning into the battlefield of Kurukshetra. Modern commentators point out the fact that Kurukshetra is not an external battlefield but one of our own making, within ourselves. It is the battlefield of life. It is not a war in the world outside ourselves, but one which we continually wage within us against the evil forces of passions, prejudices and evil inclinations, in order that we may regain the Kingdom of the Self. Arjuna was awakened enough to realize the need of struggling against these forces ; but then despondency and weakness of will got the upper hand, and he longed to fall back on the familiar ways of pleasure, which is the path of least effort. At this point of weak despair, Krishna, the voice of God, urged him to struggle further against his evil nature, and win the Kingdom of Heaven.

This explanation is in entire harmony with the teachings of the *Gita*. If the *Gita* had been a book independent of the Mahabharata, we need not have concerned ourselves with the question whether or not the war was actually fought. But since it forms a chapter of the great epic, dealing with the history of the war between the *Pandavas* and the *Kauravas,* we are forced to find a reconciliation between the fact of war and the aspiration after spiritual life as we read in the *Gita*. Ancient commentators like Sankara, Ramanuja and Sridhara took the actual war for granted. None of them made any attempt either to explain the war away, or to find reconciliation between the spirit of war and the spirit of peace ; for they all took it for granted that the readers of the *Gita* were familiar with the traditional *Dharma* of India based on caste, or gradation of life and duties. But the modern mind is not so familiar with this ancient tradition, and, moreover, it knows the worst horrors of war. Hence it finds it difficult to find justification for Krishna urging Arjuna to take part in the war.

In order, therefore, that we may perceive more clearly just why Krishna bade Arjuna fight, and how by fulfilling his duty as a warrior he could attain to the highest peace and beatitude, we must familiarize ourselves with the traditional religion of India based on the *Vedas,* and known as *Varnashramadharma* or religion and duty based on the divisions of caste and the different orders of life. The West, at least theoretically, does not believe in caste. " All men are born equal," is the social philosophy of the democratic West. Equal opportunities will bring equal results. But has this theory any basis in the facts of life ? Even supposing equality may be established on earth, would this world then remain a world ? Variety and unity in variety make up the uniform law of creation. Take away this variety, and this world would cease to be. The facts of birth and death, and of life itself, contradict the theory of equality and sameness. Since individuals are born with temperaments of different orders, they cannot grow and succeed in the same way and to the same extent, however equal might be the opportunities afforded them.

Indian philosophy does truly recognise this unity in variety. In the soul of man there is no distinction either of sex or caste, and the one God dwells in the hearts of all beings alike. In the *Gita,* as well as in the *Upanishads,* God is described as *Purusha*— one who resides in the temple of the body. But God is not expressed equally in all beings, and all beings are not equally living in God ; nor is God's power equally manifest in both Nature and man.

Sri Krishna, on the one hand, declares that ' a knower of the Self looks with an equal eye on a *Brahmana* endowed with learning and humility, a cow, an elephant, a dog and an outcaste ' (V, 18) : on the other hand he points out the difference between man and beast, as well as between man and man. And this difference is caused by the ' differentiation of *Guna* and *Karma* ' (IV, 13).

Most Indian philosophers admit the view of the *Samkhya* philosophy that the whole of Nature is composed of three forces or *Gunas,* called in Sanskrit *Sattva, Rajas* and *Tamas.* In the world of mind and matter these correspond to equilibrium, activity and inertness. *Sattva* or equilibrium is expressed by calmness, purity and tranquillity. *Rajas* or activity expresses itself in desire, power and energy. *Tamas* or inertia expresses itself as dullness, laziness and weakness.[1]

Every man has these three types of energies in him. At times *Tamas* prevails, and we are lazy ; we lose ambitions and our wills grow weak. Again *Rajas* prevails, and we become active, hopeful and ambitious, and we want to be up and doing. Or *Sattva* possesses us, as a result of which we grow calm and serene, and higher and nobler thoughts fill our minds. Though all the three forces work in each man, always one or another predominates over the other two. And a man belongs to a certain group or caste, according as which one of these forces is predominant in him.

There is no denying the fact that human society is a graded organization. Since men have different mental constitutions, one and the same ideal cannot be followed by every one in quite the same way. Swami Vivekananda has this wise remark upon the matter : " Two ways are left open to us,—the way of the ignorant, who think that there is only one way to truth and that all the rest are wrong—and the way of the wise, who admit that, according to our mental constitution or the different planes of existences in which we are, duty and morality may vary. The important thing is to know that there

---

[1] *Cf.* Plato's threefold division (Republic IV) of the soul—the rational, the spirited or concupiscent, and the temperant. These are reconciled by Justice or Righteousness. Plato may have arrived at his conclusions through study of Hindu philosophy.

are gradations of duty and morality, that the duty of one state of life, in one set of circumstances, will not and cannot be that of another."

All this does not mean, however, that the universal ideals of non-resistance, purity, non-attachment, tranquillity and the like—in short, the ideal of living in the consciousness of God—have to be adapted to the temperaments of the various people on the earth ; for the highest ideals and the supreme goal of life must ever be kept before the sight of people. But at the same time ways must be found, graded ideals must be recognized, so that everyone may gradually be enabled to follow those highest ideals.

Indian systems of morality and religion have stressed this fact from earliest times, and in the Hindu scriptures and books on ethics, different rules of conduct are formulated for different types of men. And the *Gita* insists that man should accept his ideals according to the type to which he belongs, and thus endeavour to follow his *Svadharma*—his duty according to the state of his growth. This is a surer way of progress than that of taking up other men's ideals, which can never be fully realized by one to whom they are temperamentally unsuited. "For instance," to quote Swami Vivekananda, " we take a child and at once give him the task of walking twenty miles ; either the little one dies, or one in a thousand crawls the twenty miles to reach the end, exhausted and half dead."

As a further illustration, let us consider the ideal
of non-resistance, which is the highest virtue
recognized by all the great teachers of the world.
The *Gita* also regards it as the highest ideal, but does
not assert that all people under all circumstances
must practise that virtue.   On the contrary, it points
out that for some it is necessary to learn to ' resist
evil ' in order that they may grow into a state in
which they may practise the ideal of non-resistance.
Take the concrete illustration of a man who does
not resist because he is weak or lazy, and will not
because he cannot.   Is this the virtue of non-
resistance ?   Or take another who knows that he
can strike an irresistible blow if he likes, and yet
does not strike, but blesses his enemies.   In the
words of Swami Vivekananda, " The one who from
weakness does not resist commits a sin, and as such
cannot receive any benefit from non-resistance ;
while the other would commit a sin by offering
resistance."   That is to say, we must gather the
power to resist ; then, having gained it, we must
renounce it.   Then only will this power be a
virtue.   But if we are weak and lazy, unable to
resist, and yet at the same time deceive ourselves
into the belief that we are actuated by the highest
motives, we do not merit praise.   Swami Vivekananda, admitting that the highest ideal is non-
resistance, again remarks :

" This non-resistance is the highest manifestation
of power in actual possession, and also what is called

the resisting of evil is but a step on the way towards the manifestation of this highest power, namely, non-resistance. . . . Arjuna became a coward at the sight of the mighty array against him ; his ' love ' made him forget his duty towards his country and king. That is why Sri Krishna told him that he was a hypocrite, and said, ' Thou talkest like a wise man, but thy actions betray thee to be a coward : therefore stand up and fight '."

Dr. Paul Elmer More, while reviewing the teachings of Christ, such as non-resistance, humility and renunciation, remarks : " They, if accepted by the world in their integrity, would simply make an end of the whole social fabric ; and if to these chastity be added, they would do away with human existence altogether. . . . There is every reason to believe that he (Christ) looked to see only a few chosen souls follow in his steps. "

I would add here that only a few can follow in his steps, because only a few are *Brahmanas,* with an endowment of *Sattva* in them. All others must seek graded ideals, different grades of standards and duties, in order that they may also grow to be *Brahmanas* and entirely follow the highest.

Mr. More, making a distinction between worldly and spiritual virtues, further adds : " To apply the laws of the spirit to the activities of this earth is at once a desecration and denial of religion, and a bewildering and unsettling of the social order." He declares, in effect, that as we meet other men who

are not inspired by religious virtues—and particularly is this true of social aggregates—we cannot, in
our relations with them, practise virtues like humility, purity, poverty, chastity and non-resistance in
their highest form ; for if we do, the very structure
of society would be undermined. In place of these,
he would have us practise the Aristotelian or car-
dinal virtues of justice, temperance, courage and
self-control.

The *Gita* and all Hindu books on ethics meet this
central problem of conduct in a somewhat different
way. Instead of drawing a sharp line of distinction
between virtues, worldly and spiritual, they indicate
the existence of graded virtues, different according
to the different types of humanity and their varying
conditions of life. But they insist that each is a step
leading to a virtue higher in the scale of life, and
that the ultimate goal is the attainment of spiritual
consciousness.

The *Gita* is emphatic regarding the duties and
virtues of various types of humanity. Sri Krishna
asserts that they are differentiated ' according to
the *Gunas,* born of their own nature '.

He says in the *Gita* : " Serenity of the mind, self-
control, purity, forbearance, as well as honesty,
knowledge, wisdom, belief in a hereafter—these are
virtues with which the *Brahmanas* are naturally
endowed. Heroism, bravery, fortitude, dexterity in
battle, as well as not flying from it, generosity, and
the desire for supremacy—these are natural to

Kshatriyas.   The Vaisyas are naturally inclined to
agriculture, cattle-rearing and trade ; and the Sudras
are naturally inclined to service " (XVIII, 42-44).

Since, as the *Gita* teaches, a man must follow the
duties and virtues according to the law of his own
being, he should learn to worship God through the
performance and fulfilment of his duties.   This
would ultimately help him to rise above them.   To
rise above the *Gunas,* says the *Gita,* is the highest
ideal of man.   Hence though Sri Krishna does urge
Arjuna to fulfil his duty as a Kshatriya, he wishes
him again to be *Nistraigunya*—one above the three
Gunas.   Such a process is identical with union with
Brahman or God.

In his commentary on the *Gita,* Swami Swarupa-
nanda notes as follows :   " The highest worship to
the Lord consists in the closest approach to Him.
The veil of *Maya,* comprising *Karma* or habits,
tendencies and actions, prevents a man from near-
ing the Lord, *i.e.,* realizing his own Self.   By working out one's *Karma* alone, according to the law of
one's own being, can this veil be rent and the end
accomplished."

The *Gita* furthermore explains how, through the
fulfilment of the law of one's own being, and by
offering all work and duties and virtues as worship
to the Lord, one may attain purity of heart, self-
control and dispassionateness of soul.   Then it is
that he, " renouncing all egotism, power, pride, lust,
wrath and property, freed from the idea of ' me and

mine ', and attaining tranquillity of heart, becomes
fit for realising his oneness with *Brahman* "
(XVIII, 53).

Thus human society becomes a graded organization, and as such, though the highest goal of life is
the same for all men, and certain truths are universal, these matters of highest import cannot be
attained by all in precisely the same way. The
special requirement of individuals—their varying
natures, tendencies, temperaments—must be recognized, and man has to be treated as a ' spiritual
being in the process of formation '. Hence the
necessity of an accepted scripture or a spiritual
teacher to provide the right means by which a person
may understand those graded ideals which would
help him, according to the law of his own life and
being, to move towards his spiritual development
and self-perfection.

III

The *Upanishads,* as we have learned, gave the
Law of Karma and Reincarnation. philosophy of *Karma* and re-birth
a central place in their teachings,
and this is true of the *Gita* also. It
was in fact during the Epic Period, to which the
Gita belongs, that this doctrine received its greatest
emphasis and attained its fullest development. Sub-
sequently, all systems of thought, including Jainism
and Buddhism, incorporated this theory into their

teachings with but slight variations, indeed, it has become the basic universal principle in all Indian thought. It is especially true that many of the verses of the *Gita* make reference to the doctrine in a most illuminating manner.

Karma is a Sanskrit word meaning work or action. In a broader sense this word includes thoughts as well. Thus both thoughts and actions, whether conscious, subconscious, or reflex, can be included in the term *Karma*. After an act is done and forgotten, it is not altogether lost, for it produces thought waves, which in turn, subside and remain in the subconscious region of the mind as impressions. A deed is done and forgotten, but the mental impression, called *Samskara,* remains. Memory is the process of recalling to the conscious mind these subconscious impressions. Countless such impressions are stored up in the subconscious mind, some of which may at our will issue forth into conscious thought. The sum total of these impressions forms one's individual character, and this character guides one's motives and conduct as well as future thought and action. Thus every *Karma* becomes the seed of another *Karma.* So every *Karma,* good or bad, is both cause and effect, just as every action produces reaction in the form of experience of happiness or misery according to the nature of the thought or deed, whether it be good or evil.

Philosophically the word *Karma* signifies the law of causation. In science this law is applied to the physical universe. Indian philosophy applies it to the mental and moral planes as well, as the just law of compensation and of retribution. "As a man soweth, so shall he reap," we read in the Hebrew scriptures. Manu, the law-giver of India, declares, "Thou canst not gather what thou dost not sow. As thou dost plant the tree, so will it grow."[1]

Our enjoyments and our sufferings, our knowledge and our ignorance, our experiences of happiness or misery, are of our own making—the effects of our good or evil *Karmas*. And it follows that our characters are our own creations.

Kant, the German philosopher, in discussing the moral order of the universe, says very truly that happiness is the result of virtuous deeds, and suffering arises from sin. Then, in pointing to the actual facts as they exist in this world, he declares that want of virtue does not result in want of happiness, nor is virtue always unaccompanied by suffering. He explains the apparent injustice in this contrarity by admitting that the soul continues to exist after death, and that in the next world justice is meted out, the virtuous being rewarded with happiness and the sinful punished with suffering. This he calls the postulate of Practical Reason.

[1] The Greek idea of Nemesis has its origin in some phase of this law of retribution, which finds recognition in nearly all the religions of the world.

Thus one great Western philosopher assumes a moral universe in which the law of justice and compensation operates through the continuity of the soul after death. But does the admission of a future life explain the injustices of the present life ? Why should a good man suffer in this world ? That his sufferings are the effect of some deeds is also admitted by Kant. Why then seek the cause in some after-life ? The cause cannot follow the effect, but the effect invariably follows the cause. The Indian law of *Karma* or causation assumes not only the continuity of the soul in a future life but also its continuity from a beginningless past.

Sri Krishna pertinently says : " Many are the births that have been passed through by Me and thee, O Arjuna. I know them all, whilst thou knowest not (IV, 5). It is not that I have never existed, nor thou, nor these kings. Nor is it that we shall cease to exist in the future " (II, 12).

Therefore, our present life, with all its joys and its sufferings, with all its inborn tendencies, is the result of our *Karmas* in our past lives. Metaphysically, *Karma* is divided into three classes—*Kriyamana* or the deeds of the present life, *Samchita* or stored-up *Karmas,* and *Prarabdha* or the stored-up *Karmas* of the past which unfold in the present life. In our present life we are creating new *Karmas* known as *Kriyamana.* Some deeds bear fruit either immediately or later in this present life itself. All do not, however, bear fruits in the same

life but become Samchita or stored-up *Karmas.*
And from many past lives we carry the *Samchita*
or stored-up *Karmas,* some of which in turn become
Prarabdha, as we reap the effect of past deeds in
the present life. Our present life and many of
our current experiences are the effects of our
Prarabdha.

This law of *Karma* is the only valid explanation of
the moral order of the universe. If we do not admit
the fact of pre-existence, and instead hold to the
theory of first birth, we can have no explanation of
the inequality and manifold mysteries of the world,
unless of course we admit of a God who is responsi-
ble for such a state of things—which is no explanation at all. On this point Samkara the great Indian
philosopher, says : " Passion and malice would
have to be ascribed to God, which attributes would
be contrary to the essential goodness of the Lord.
. . . The fact is that beings are born according
to their merits and demerits in the past." Again he
says : " The position of the Lord is to be looked
upon as analogous to that of *Parjanya,* the giver of
rain. For as *Parjanya* is the common cause of the
production of rice, barley and other plants, while
the difference between the various species is due to
the potentialities lying hidden in the respective
seeds, so the Lord is the common cause of the
creation of gods, men, etc., while the differences
between these classes of beings are due to the
difference in the merit belonging to the individual

9

souls. Hence the Lord cannot be reproached with inequality of dispensation and cruelty."[1]

The law of *Karma* is generally identified with fatalism or determinism by mistake ; for according to this law our actions as well as our wills are to a certain degree determined by our character. It is true that a man has imposed upon himself the limitation of his own character as determined by his *Karmas,* but at the same time he is free either to follow the tendency formed by the past or to struggle against it. This faculty of choosing is the function of the will, which possesses freedom. *Karma* implies a free doer. The law of *Karma* therefore postulates that every man is placed in charge of himself by the fact of self-consciousness. Buddhism, for example, though it stresses the law of *Karma,* at every point urges self-exertion. And the *Gita*

[1] An objection may be raised that the words, ' Being only was in the beginning, one without a second ', affirms that before the creation there was no distinction and consequently no merit on account of which creation might have become unequal. And if we assume the Lord to have been guided in His dispensations by the actions of living beings subsequent to their creation, we involve ourselves in the circular reasoning that work depends on diversity of condition of life, and diversity of condition again on work. The Lord may be considered as acting with regard to religious merit after distinction had once risen ; but as before that, the cause of inequality, viz., merit, did not exist, it follows that the first creation must have been free from inequalities.

"This objection we meet by the remark that the transmigratory world is without beginning. The objection would be valid if the world had a beginning ; but as it is without beginning, merit and inequality are, like seed and sprout, caused as well as causes, and there is therefore no logical objection to their operation."—Samkara's commentary on the *Vedanta Sutras,* translated by G. Thibaut.

teaches that ' the self is to be saved by one's own self. The self alone is either the friend of the self or the enemy of the self ' (VI, 5).

Another charge is often brought against the law of *Karma,* namely, that it leaves no room for social service. If each man's pleasure or pain is of his own making, the direct result of his deeds or misdeeds, why should another interfere to mitigate his suffering ?

On the contrary, the law of *Karma* implies that if, in spite of having the power to relieve another's suffering, a person does not exercise it, he creates a bad *Karma* for himself ; and that when a man in pain finds help, he finds help also because of his own good deed. Thus the law urges every man to perform good deeds and to exert himself to overcome his own misdeeds.

We have already seen how the law of *Karma* establishes the moral order of the universe by admitting not only the continuity of the soul in the future but also its pre-existence. Psychologically, it alone offers the explanation of the possibility of gaining experience in this our present life. No knowledge is possible without previous experience. If, as Locke contended, the mind in the beginning is a ' tabula rasa ', a blank sheet of paper, then the mind would always remain in that state. Western psychologists and scientists of to-day also point out that children are born endowed with previous knowledge, which they call instinct. Herbert Spencer

declares that if a child one month old is observed
attentively, his individual character may be distinguished. Whence came this instinct and this
character ? Western psychologists ascribe it to
heredity, but Dr. August Weismann, the great
scientist, disproves this theory of heredity by showing that ' an organism cannot acquire anything
unless it has the pre-disposition to acquire it. . . .
Nothing can arise in an organism unless the pre-
disposition to it is pre-existent, for every acquired
characteristic is simply the reaction of the organism
upon a certain stimulus.'

Having proved that instinct and character are not
directly inherited from parents—for there must
pre-exist the pre-disposition in the child—the learned
doctor finds himself at a loss to explain wherefrom
the child receives its pre-disposition, and he falls
back, therefore on the theory that tendencies and
peculiarities are inherited ' from the common stock ',
a vague conclusion leading us to the same dilemma
as before, *i.e.*, whence and how did the ' common
stock ' begin to exist ?

The Indian philosophers argue that these tendencies, and what are known as instincts, are acquired
by the child itself in previous incarnations, and that
the soul has existed from a beginningless past. For
these philosophers say that our experiences cannot
be annihilated. Our *Karmas,* though apparently
disappearing, remain still unperceived (*Adrishta*),
and reappear in their effect as *Pravritti* or

tendencies. Swami Vivekananda summarises the matter thus :

" So far as explaining the tendencies of the present life by past conscious efforts goes, the reincarnationists of India and the latest school of evolutionists are at one. The only difference is that the Hindus, as spiritualists, explain it by the conscious efforts of individual souls, and the materialistic school of evolutionists explain it by hereditary physical transmission. The schools which hold to the theory of creation out of nothing, are entirely out of court.

" The issue has to be fought out between the reincarnationists who hold that all experiences are stored up as tendencies in the subject of those experiences, the individual soul, and are transmitted by reincarnation of that unbroken individuality— and the materialists who hold that the brain is the subject of all actions and adopt the theory of transmission through cells.

" It is thus the doctrine of reincarnation assumes an infinite importance to our mind, for the fight between reincarnation and mere cellular transmission is, in reality, the fight between spiritualism and materialism. If cellular transmission is the all-sufficient explanation, materialism is inevitable, and there is no necessity for the theory of a soul. If it is not a sufficient explanation, the theory of an individual soul bringing into this life the experiences of the past, is absolutely true. There is no escape from the alternative, reincarnation or materialism. Which shall we accept ? "

One objection brought against the theory of pre-existence is that we do not remember our past. But is memory the criterion of existence ? Does the fact that we do not remember the days of our infancy prove that we did not exist as infants ? Whether we remember them or not, the sum total of our experiences in the past reappears in the form of tendencies in our present. Furthermore, some exceptional children are born with memories of past birth. These are called *Jatismaras*—born with memories of a past life. Instances are not wanting of such children in every age. Patanjali, father of *Yoga* philosophy, explains how by a certain process of *Yoga* memory of the past may be revived by any one who will submit to its discipline.[1]

[1] (*a*) *Cf.* Tennyson's sense of this recurrence of the past in *The Two Voices* :

> Or, if through lower lives I came—
> Tho' all experiences past became
> Consolidate in mind and frame—
> I might forget my weaker lot ;
> For is not our first year forgot ?
> The haunts of memory echo not.

(*b*) Other Western philosophers, scientists and poets have echoed the belief in pre-existence and reincarnation. In Plato's Phaedo, above all, one of the characters says, " Your favourite doctrine, Socrates, that knowledge is simply recol-lection, if true, also necessarily implies a previous time in which we learned that which we now recollect. But this would be impossible unless our soul was in some place before existing in the human form ; here then is another argument for the soul's immortality." And the beautiful dialogue, conducted by Socrates with his friends just before

The *Gita,* like the *Upanishads,* teaches that the soul is unborn and undying ; for birth and death are attributes of the body and of the mind, and not of the soul.   It declares :   " Unborn, eternally existent, changeless, ever Itself—is this Self.   He who knows his Self to be indestructible, changeless, without birth, and immutable, how is he to slay or cause the slaying of another ? (II, 20, 21).   This Self, weapons cut not ; This, fire burns not ; This, water wets not ; and This, wind dries not (II, 23).   Changeless, all-pervading, unmoving, immovable, the Self is eternal " (II, 24).

he drank the hemlock, has to do with this very matter of rebirth and reincarnation.   See also the myth related at the conclusion of *The Republic.*

(*c*) " If ye will receive it, this is Elias, which was for to come."—*Matt. XI,* 14.

(*d*) " I think this is a question how it happens that the human mind is influenced now by good, now by evil.   The causes of this I suspect to be more ancient than this cor- poreal birth."—Origen, a Church Father who lived before the Council of Nicaea.

(*e*) " Is this hypothesis so laughable merely because it is the oldest ? because the human understanding, before the sophistries of the schools had dissipated and debilitated it, lighted upon it at once ?   Why should not I come back as often as I am capable of acquiring fresh knowledge, fresh experience ?   Do I bring away so much from one experience that there is nothing to repay the trouble of coming back ? "—Lessing.

(*f*)" None but hasty thinkers will reject it (reincarna- tion) on the ground of inherent absurdity.   Like the doctrine of evolution itself, that of transmigration has its roots in the world of reality."—Thomas H. Huxley.

(*g*) " We wake and find ourselves on a stairs.   There are stairs below us which we seem to have ascended ; there are stairs above us, many a one, which go upward and out of sight."—R. W. Emerson.

What are death and re-birth? The *Gita* says: "As are childhood, youth and old age in this body to the embodied soul, so also is the attaining of another body (II, 13). Even as a man casts off worn-out clothes, and puts on others which are new, so the embodied casts off worn-out bodies, and enters into others which are new" (II, 22).[1]

When we realise the soul as the innermost Self, as the indestructible and unchangeable reality within us, then it is that for us birth and death cease to be. The soul reincarnates only so long as it remains ignorant of its real nature and therefore of God. In the words of the *Gita* : "Reaching the highest perfection, and having attained Me, the great-souled ones are no more subject to re-birth—the home of pain and ephemeral living. All the worlds, including the realm of *Brahma,* are subject to return but after attaining Me, there is no re-birth" (VIII, 15-16).

But if there is no re-birth for these great-souled ones, what becomes of their *Karmas*? The law of *Karma,* as we have already learned, necessitates re-birth that the succession of *Karmas* may fructify ;

[1] *Cf.* "Death, so-called, is but other
matter dress'd
In some new form. And in a
varied vest,
From tenement to tenement
though toss'd,
The soul is still the same,
The figure only lost.

—*Poem on Pythagoras,* Dryden's *Ovid.*

that is, as we create new *Karma,* all of which do not take effect in this life, and as there are in addition other stored-up *Karmas* which have not yet germinated in the present, there would seem to be an unfulfilled termination of this law if there is no re-birth. Where then is the effect for which there is a logical cause ? How can one break the chain of causation ?

To this problem Indian philosophy offers a rational solution in the statement that *Karma* attaches itself to the mind and not to the real Self which is above impurity and attachment. The effects of *Karma* are therefore realized so long as the individual ego exists, so long as through ignorance the Self is identified with mind and body. The moment one attains to knowledge of the true Self, the law of *Karma* no longer operates for him ; for he overcomes all *Karma* and re-birth. Thus the *Gita* says : " As blazing fire reduces fuel to ashes, so does the fire of knowledge reduce all *Karma* to ashes. Verily there exists nothing in this world so purifying as knowledge. In good time, having reached perfection in Yoga, one realizes one's self in one's own heart " (IV, 37, 38).

Sridhara Swami, a noted commentator on the *Gita,* however, exempts from that blazing fire of knowledge which reduces all *Karmas* to ashes, the *Prarabdha* or the part of the stored-up past *Karma* which has begun to germinate in this present life. Samkara, who preceded him by many centuries holds the same view as is evident from his commentary on the passage quoted. These authoritative views make it clear that *Prarabdha* can be exhausted only by being worked out, in this present life.

The *Sankya* philosopher, Kapila, further explains how the *Prarabdha* works itself out in a free soul, an enlightened one, like the momentum of an automaton when the operator has left it running. Eventually it runs down and stops of its own accord. All other *Karmas* are like unto burned seeds.

But there still remain the new *Karmas* created after enlightenment. What of them ? The *Gita* declares that these do not affect the free soul, for the soul is no longer possessed by the ego. It says : " He who has nothing more to hope for, he who is self-controlled, and who has renounced all possessions, he does not suffer the consequences by mere bodily action. Content with what comes to him without effort, unaffected by the pairs of opposites, free from envy, even-minded in success and failure, though acting, he is not bound " (IV, 21, 22). " With the mind purified by devotion to performance of action, and with the body conquered and senses subdued, one who realises one's self as the Self of all beings, though acting, is not tainted " (V, 7).

Thus, just as in the *Vedic* scriptures, the supreme goal of life held forth by the *Gita* is the knowledge of Self or God, and the attainment of freedom from *Karma* and re-birth.

IV

As we have already learned, the supreme goal of
Is Nirvana Compatible with Works in the World ? human life is *Moksha* or liberation. It is in effect the release from the wheel of birth and death through the attainment of knowledge of the true Self which is one with *Brahman*. It is also complete cessation of pain and sorrow. As already explained, our sufferings are immediate experiences, and, as such, the immediate and direct experience of the Self in union with the blissful *Brahman* can alone free us from all our suffering. This ideal of *Moksha* is called in the *Gita* as *Brahma-nirvana*— extinction in *Brahman* or union with *Brahman*. It exactly corresponds to attaining the Kingdom of Heaven within. Christ teaches us, " Be ye perfect even as the Father in Heaven is perfect." The same ideal of perfection is taught in the *Gita* as attainable in this very life. *Moksha* (salvation) or *Brahma-nirvana* (Heaven) is not a post-mortem experience, but one to be attained here and now. And every age produces living souls that do attain *Nirvana* in this life. In the words of the *Gita* : " With the heart unattached to external objects, he realizes the joy that is in the Self. Such a one attains the undecaying happiness, for his self is in constant union with *Brahman* " (V, 21).

" With imperfections exhausted, doubts dispelled, senses controlled, with an interest in the good of all beings, the *Rishis* attain *Nirvana* in *Brahman*. Released from lust and anger, with the heart controlled and the Self realized, such great ones find *Brahma-nirvana,* both here and hereafter " (V, 25-26).

Thus the *Gita* teaches that through *Yogic* practices of non-attachment, and through freedom from lust and anger, one attains purity and perfection and everlasting peace (the peace that passeth all understanding) while still living in this world. This means that complete cessation of miseries and perfect freedom can be won here upon earth to be enjoyed in our earthly life. For according to the *Gita,* " He who has inner happiness, who has repose within and light within, that *Yogi* becomes one with *Brahman* as he attains *Nirvana* or self-extinction in *Brahman* " (V, 24).

Nirvana or self-extinction in *Brahman* clearly implies extinction of the ego, the false self, in the higher spiritualized Self—the basis of all knowledge, of all existence, and of all happiness. One no longer identifies oneself with the limitations of the body, the senses and the mind, but unites oneself in consciousness with *Brahman,* the all-pervading and divine existence. This consciousness is the transcendental consciousness which is beyond outer consciousness—the *Samadhi* of the *Yogis,* the *Nirvana* of the Buddhists, and the Kingdom of Heaven of the Christians. One does not, however, dwell in that state of complete absorption without cessation. He returns to normal consciousness when he is in contact with what we may call outer-world-consciousness, but the illumination which he experienced in the transcendental state never again leaves him. Though he is now experiencing the world, and is vividly conscious of the manifold universe, he knows his true Self, and the sense of the Divine Presence is ever with him. We read in the *Gita* : " With the heart gathered to itself by *Yoga*, with the eye of evenness for all things, he beholds the Self in all beings, and all beings in the Self. He who sees Me in all things, and sees all things in Me, he is never separated from Me, nor am I separated from him " (VI, 29, 30).

Thus we comprehend that the illumination derived from the transcendental experience is not confined to the state of actual absorption, but extends beyond into the normal state of multiplicity of the changing world. But one who has had that experience sees the relative universe with an eye of evenness ; for, though he perceives multiplicity and relativity, and the concomitant play of joys and sorrows, of life and death, yet he sees present behind the relativity and the multiplicity—the one, immutable, blissful *Brahman*. It is then, affirms the *Gita,* that he discovers a love for all his fellows and creates the will to do them good.

Thus *Nirvana* is clearly compatible with worldly activity. In practice also we see in the lives of Krishna, Buddha, Christ, Samkara, Ramakrishna,

Vivekananda, and many others how, having attained to transcendental consciousness, they continued to pass illumined lives in the service of humanity. But this humanitarian service is first of all founded on the love of God—a love which perceives all men in the being of God.

More than all the sacred scriptures of the world, the *Gita* insists on action in the world, and exhorts men never to cease from activity and the doing of good to others. We shall see, when we come to discuss *Karma Yoga,* how works aid in self-purification and the attainment of *Brahma-nirvana.* Having reached perfection in *Yoga,* one ceases not from action, though one has nothing more to gain from works.

The charge brought against Indian religions, especially Buddhism, that they inculcate passivity and inaction, is without any real basis. Both Hinduism and Buddhism have as their ideal *Nirvana,* or the attainment of the Kingdom of Heaven, which is an experience of unalloyed bliss in God while one continues to live a life of intense activity in this world of flux and multiplicity, knowing the one God behind this world of appearances.

One very pertinent question, however, arises in this connection. The *Brahma-nirvana* of the *Gita* as well as the *Nirvana* of Buddhism clearly means the extinction of the ego and the realization of the transcendental consciousness, or state of attainment beyond external consciousness ; but as one returns

from the transcendental state to normal consciousness, does not his former ego-consciousness return
to him ? Without this consciousness, how is it possible again to perceive the multiple universe or perform any service to humanity ?

Sri Ramakrishna, to whom *Samadhi* or transcendental consciousness may be said to have been as
natural as is normal consciousness to us, and who
yet continued to live for the good of humanity,
explained this problem in his simple way as
follows :

"Some retain the sense of ego as 'the servant I'
or 'the devotee I'—the sense 'Thou art the Lord.
I am Thy child'—even after attaining *Samadhi*.
The 'I' of a devotee does no harm to any living
creature. It is like a sword which, after touching the
Philosophers' Stone, is turned to gold. The sword
retains the same form but it does not cut or injure
anyone. The dry leaves of the cocoanut tree drop
off in the wind, leaving marks on the trunk ; those
marks only show that there were leaves there at one
time. Similarly, only the form or mark of ego is
left in one who has reached God. Also his passions
remain only as empty forms. He becomes simple
and pure like a child.

"Samkara and spiritual teachers like him came
down to the consciousness of 'ego' for the teaching
and good of humanity. The bee buzzes until it
alights in the heart of the flower. It becomes silent
as soon as it begins to drink the honey. Then again,

after it has drunk its fill, it makes a sweet humming sound.

" Few can stay long on the roof. Those who reach *Samadhi* and attain *Brahman* return to the lower plane of consciousness and then realize that it is He who has become man and the universe. The singer cannot hold to the highest note very long. He comes down to the lower notes. Similarly, the man of realization comes back from the transcendental consciousness and perceives the world of relativity, and, though he sees the world, he sees *Brahman* everywhere."

A liberated man, as we saw in discussing the law of *Karma,* overcomes the world of *Karmas,* and though he continues to live and work, he is not bound or tainted by *Karmas.* And he lives only to exhaust the Prarabdha Karmas.[1] After he has exhausted his *Prarabdha,* the body falls away and he attains what is known as absolute freedom. The state of mind of the free soul at death is thus described in the *Gita* :   " Remembering whatever object, at the end, he leaves the body, that alone is reached by him, because of his constant thought of the object " (VIII, 6). This is the general law : a man's

---

[1] In the teachings of the *Gita,* however, a distinction is made between the *Avataras* or Divine Incarnations such as Krishna, Christ and others on the one hand, and ordinary souls who attain *Nirvana* through struggles of their own, on the other. The former have no *Prarabdhas* and have never been subject to the law of *Karma* ; the latter free themselves from all *Karmas* except the *Prarabdha,* and this part of the *Karma* they work out and attain absolute freedom at death.

next life is guided by his present one ; the sum total
of his deeds in the present life, the attachment or
desire that has been his, comes to his mind before
death and determines his immediate future existence. And this same law applies to a free soul
whose only love and attachment has been God. So
it is said, he goes to Him.

Thus we read in the *Gita* : " With the mind not
moving towards anything else, made steadfast by
the method of habitual meditation, and dwelling in
the supreme, resplendent *Purusha,* one goes to
Him (VIII, 8). Controlling all the senses, confining
the mind in the heart, drawing the *Prana* into the
head, occupied in the practice of concentration,
uttering the one syllable *Om,* the *Brahman,* and
meditating on Me, he who departs, leaving the body,
attains the supreme goal (VIII, 12, 13). Reaching
the highest perfection, and having attained Me, the
great-souled ones are no more subject to re-birth
which is sorrowful and impermanent " (VIII, 15).
This is known as absolute freedom.

The *Gita* raises one more problem, this time with
reference to the man who struggles to attain perfection and fails to realize it in this life. Perhaps the
following extended quotation will best explain the
problem :

Arjuna said : " Though possessed of *Shraddha*
but unable to control himself, with the mind wandering away from *Yoga,* what end does one, failing
to gain perfection in *Yoga,* meet, O Krishna ? Does

10

he not, fallen from both, perish, without support, like
a rent cloud, deluded in the path of *Brahman* ? "

The Blessed Lord replied : " Verily there is destruction for him, neither here nor hereafter ; for
the doer of good never comes to grief. Having
attained to the world of the righteous[1], and dwelling there for long years, the fallen in *Yoga* reincarnate in the home of the pure and the prosperous.
Or else he is born into a family of wise *Yogis* only ;
verily, a birth such as that is very rare to obtain in
this world. There he is united with the intelligence
acquired in his former body, and strives more than
before, for perfection. By that previous practice
alone he is borne on in spite of himself. The *Yogi*,
striving assiduously, purified of heart, gaining perfection through many births, reaches the highest
goal " (VI, 37-45).

V

In its analysis of the Ultimate Reality, the *Gita*

The Ultimate
Reality : God
and Avatara.

brings out explicitly what is implied
in the direct experiences of the
seers and sages of the *Upanishads*.
Behind the following objects of this phenomenal

---

[1] The worlds of the righteous refer to the heavens—the
spheres of enjoyment. The Hindus have the conception of
heavens and heavenly enjoyments which one experiences
after death ; but according to all Indian philosophy, to go
to such heavens is not the supreme goal. One may go
there to enjoy the fruits of one's good deeds ; but after the
exhaustion of the good deeds accumulated during earthly
existence, one reincarnates again in the world.

world lies a changeless, permanent reality, the Supreme Brahman ; and behind the fleeting body, senses and mind of an individual human being is the Self, also a changeless, permanent reality ; and this Self is one with Supreme Self. Every individual houses within himself the Eternal Spirit, the immutable, timeless Self-existence ; and though He dwells within all, and all beings exist in Him, He is not tainted or affected by the thoughts and actions, good or evil, of individual men. " The Omnipresent takes note of the merit or fault of none. Knowledge is enveloped in ignorance, hence do beings become deluded. But where ignorance is destroyed by the knowledge of the Self, that knowledge, like the sun, reveals the Supreme *Brahman* " (V, 14, 15).

This knowledge of the immutable, eternal, timeless Self-existence is, as we have already seen, called *Brahma-nirvana*. It is not, however, to be confused with intellectual concepts, nor understood to be a method of thinking. It is a direct, immediate experience, in which, as Sri Ramakrishna once told his disciple Vivekananda, the spiritualized consciousness sees God more directly, more intimately, than the physical consciousness experiences the objective world.[1]

Is it then possible to define this experience of God ? The *Gita* affirms that His Svarupa or true

[1] *Cf.* Plato's distinction between knowledge and opinion —(*Republic* IV).

being is unthinkable, indefinable, and yet realisable. For it says : " He who knows My true being, he amongst mortals is liberated from ignorance and bondage of sin."

Sri Ramakrishna says : " When one attains *Samadhi,* then alone comes the knowledge of *Brahman,* and one attains the vision of God. In that ecstatic realization, all thoughts cease, and one becomes perfectly silent. There is no power of speech left by which to express *Brahman.* For verily is He beyond thought and speech."

The method adopted by the philosophic mind of India to determine the Indeterminable has been the process of negation—*Neti Neti Atman, " Atman* is neither this nor that." In the case of Buddha we find he did not attempt even this negative way of defining. He always remained silent when questioned about the undefinable. But the *Gita* admits that this difficult and abstract method of negation can be followed only by a select few of exceptional nature and training. " But those who worship the Imperishable, the Indefinable, the Unmanifested, the Omnipresent, the Unthinkable, the Unchangeable, the Immovable, the Eternal, having subdued all their senses, even-minded everywhere, and devoted to the welfare of all beings,—verily, they reach Myself alone. Greater is their trouble whose minds are set on the Unmanifested, for the goal of the Unmanifested is very hard for the embodied to reach " (XII, 3, 4, 5).

So, because of the arduous nature of the path to
Godhead, we find in the *Gita,* as well as in the
Upanishads, not merely the abstract conception of
an Absolute who is merely the Beyond, but a God
who is ' the Father, the Mother, the Sustainer of the
world' (IX, 17). We find an ideal of God in the
Gita, who is ' the Goal, the Supporter, the Lord, the
Witness, the Abode, the Refuge, the Friend, the
Origin, the Dissolution, the Substratum, the Store-
house, the Seed immutable' (IX, 18),—thus answer-
ing the need of a human heart, the need for love
and work and worship.

This conception of an Impersonal-Personal God
which we find in the teachings of the Indian
scriptures is not new, nor is it the fruit of human
reason. Indeed most Hindu thinkers do not believe
that the proofs of the existence of God lie in the
realm of our reason, but rather in the fact of His
realization, in the experience of seing Him and
realizing Him in His Fulness. Both these aspects
of Godhead—the Personal as well as the Impersonal
—are realized and experienced by those whose
divine sight has been opened.

Sri Ramakrishna, the greatest mystic philosopher
of our age, having realized God in all His aspects
utters this truth concerning the conception of an
Impersonal-Personal Godhead, which is revealed in
the *Gita* as well. He says : " The *Jnani* or one of
philosophic mind analyses the universe of senses,
saying, ' *Brahman* is not this, not that', and gives up

all worldliness. Thus does he reach the knowledge of *Brahman,* just as the man who climbs a stairway leaves each step behind and so reaches the roof. But the *Vijnani* who gains an intimate knowledge of Him has his consciousness extended. He knows that the roof and the steps are all made of the same substance. He who is realized as *Brahman,* by following the process of elimination, is also realized as becoming man and the universe. The *Vijnani,* the man of higher realization, knows that He who is without attributes in one aspect is, in another aspect, the repository of all blessed attributes.

" The true knower knows that He who is *Brahman* is God ; He who is impersonal, attributeless and beyond the *Gunas,* is again the Personal God, the repository of all blessed qualities. Man, the universe, mind, intelligence, love, dispassion, knowledge—these are the expressions of His power and glory " (*Sri Ramakrishna Kathamrita* in Bengali by M.).

The conception of a Personal God, as explained in the *Gita,* has been identified by certain modern Indian thinkers with theism whereas some Western writers have called that conception of Godhead by the name of pantheism. But it would be a great mistake to identify the teachings of the *Gita* with phases of Western ' isms '. God, to Hindu thinkers, is not a mere intellectual abstraction, nor a mode of thinking ; He is a Being realized and realizable. Western theism and pantheism are at their best intellectual concepts, or convictions of the mind, whereas God, as has been clearly revealed in all Hindu scriptures, is beyond mind and thought. When this Being beyond thought is given by the seers a name within the domain of thought, this name appears like theism or pantheism, yet He remains vastly different from the intellectualised God of the West. On this point Aurobindo, who, perhaps of all modern interpreters of the *Gita,* has best caught the spirit of the poem, says :

" . . . it is no shrinking and gingerly theism afraid of the world's contradictions, but one which sees God as the omniscient and omnipotent, the sole original Being who manifests in himself all, whatever it may be, good and evil, pain and pleasure, light and darkness as stuff of his own existence and governs himself what in himself he has manifested. Unaffected by its oppositions, unbound by his creation, exceeding, yet intimately related to this Nature and closely one with her creatures, their Spirit, Self, highest Soul, Lord, Lover, Friend, Refuge, he is ever leading them from within them and from above through the mortal appearances of ignorance and suffering and sin and evil, ever leading each through his nature and all through universal nature towards a supreme light and bliss and immortality and transcendence. This is the fulness of the liberating knowledge. It is a knowledge of the Divine within us and in the world as at the same time a transcendent Infinite. An Absolute who has become all that is by his divine Nature, his effective powers of Spirit, he governs all from his transcendence. He is intimately present within every creature and the cause, ruler, director of all cosmic happenings and yet is he far too great, mighty and infinite to be limited by his creation "—(*Essays on the Gita by* Sri Aurobindo, Second Series, pp. 133-134).

The ideal of a Personal God is certainly present in the *Gita,* but it is an ideal of an Impersonal-Personal Deity, expressing ultimate Oneness in which there exists no ' I ' or ' Thou ' but only the one impartible, self-luminous, blissful Existence. This truth of absorption in the Absolute and perfect union by identity, from which the devotee, preoccupied too exclusively with some Divine Personality and in the values of the finite world, may at first shrink, is however borne witness to by the mystic experiences of the sages and devotees. Be they a St. Francis of Assisi or a Sri Chaitanya of Bengal, though they may begin their life of devotion by loving and worshipping a Personal God, they conclude it by realising their oneness with the Eternal and by being absorbed in Him.

In the same way the teachings of Christ, or of the Bible as a whole cannot be identified with any of the theological conceptions of Godhead, either theistic or pantheistic, in spite of all apparent resemblances with them. When Christ bids us pray to the Father in Heaven, we can give his words a theistic or deistic interpretation ; but when he indicates that

the Kingdom of God is within, and that ' I and my
Father are one ', he gives to the whole a mystic
implication not usually understood by the word
' theism '. And in the 139th Psalm occur the following words of great mystic significance :

"Whither shall I go from Thy spirit ? Or whither
shall I flee from Thy presence ? If I ascend up into
Heaven, Thou art there ; if I make my bed in hell,
behold, Thou art there. If I take the wings of the
morning, and dwell in the uttermost parts of the
sea, even there shall Thy hand lead me, and Thy
right hand shall hold me."

Just as the idea of one, immutable God, personal
and yet impersonal in His nature, pervades all
advanced religions, so the conception of an *Avatara,*
the Supreme Being descending upon earth in
human form, seems also to be universal. This conception finds its place for the first time in Indian
philosophy in the *Gita,* though its basis is laid in
certain passages of the *Upanishads.* That God dwells
in the hearts of all beings as their innermost Self,
is the fundamental truth of both these scriptures.
To know that innermost Self is to become one with
God. "A knower of *Brahman* becomes *Brahman,*"
declare the seers of the *Upanishads.* Since God
exists in all beings, every being in a sense is a
descent from God into the finiteness of name and
form, and only the veil of ignorance hides its
essential identity ; but when one is born with the
full knowledge of the Self, and with the Divine

consciousness not veiled by ignorance, that being appears to be a full embodiment of the Godhead. Such a man is known as an *Avatara*.

The *Gita* doctrine of Avatara is parallel and almost identical with the conception of the Word made flesh, ' full of grace and truth ', as we find it in the Gospel according to St. John,[1] but with this difference, that Jesus of Nazareth has alone been identified with the Logos, the only begotten Son of God (John 3 : 16), whereas in the *Gita* it is clearly stated that He is made flesh many times, in different ages and in different forms. It is thus easy for Hindus to accept Christ as one of the *Avataras* of Godhead, and they may unreservedly worship Him in the same way in which they worship Krishna. They cannot, however, understand Christ as the only Son of God, and they do not accept Him as such a being.

Krishna, the teacher of the *Gita,* openly declares himself to be the Incarnation of the Godhead, asserting that He had passed through many incarnations whenever He was needed upon earth. " Many are the births that have been passed by Me and thee, O Arjuna. I know them all, while thou knowest not " (IV, 5). His birth, however, is not similar to those of Arjuna and other embodied souls, who are born in consequence of their past *Karmas,* are tied by the fetters of ignorance, and remain under the

[1] " In the beginning was the Word, and the Word was with God, and the Word was God." *John,* 1 : 1.

thraldom of *Maya*. The birth of a Krishna or a Christ
or a Ramakrishna does not lie under the weight
of past *Karmas* but is the result of free choice ; for
the Incarnation does not yield to the domination of
Maya but rather puts it under subjection, does not
live in ignorance but in full consciousness of his divinity. " Though I am unborn, of changeless nature,
and the Lord of beings, yet subjugating My *Prakriti,*
I come into being by My own *Maya* " (IV, 6).

Sri Krishna continues : " He who thus knows, in
true light, My divine birth and action, leaving the
body is not born again : he attains to Me, O
Arjuna."

Compare these with the words of the *Bible* : " But
as many as received Him, to them gave He power
to become the sons of God ; even to them that
believe on His name " (*St. John*, 1 : 12).

To know or to receive a Krishna or a Christ or a
Ramakrishna is to know God ; for verily these are
the children of Light, Light themselves. Swami
Vivekananda has remarked that the vibrations of
light are everywhere, even in darkness, but to see
a light, one must look through an electric bulb.
Similarly though God dwells everywhere, to see
Him, one must look through these children of Light.
To worship a Krishna or a Christ is not, however,
to worship a man as God, is not to worship a per-
son ; it is to worship God Himself, the Impersonal-
Personal Existence in and through a man-god. Sri
Ramakrishna said that the Divine Incarnations are

like so many doors through which we peep into or touch the Infinite.

Avatarhood, therefore, is not limited to one personality but manifests itself through many incarnations. " Freed from attachment, fear and anger, absorbed in Me, taking refuge in Me, purified by the fire of knowledge, many have attained My Being " (IV, 10).

Thus Sri Krishna makes it clear that this ' I ' or ' Me ' is not limited to himself, one man-god. Moreover, he declares :

" In whatever way men worship Me, in the same way do I fulfil their desires ; it is My path that men tread, in all ways " (IV, 11).

The *Gita* also describes the conditions which necessitate the birth of Divine Incarnations. The Hindus have a theory, demonstrated by historical events, that spiritual culture moves in cyclic waves. There is an upward movement which is followed by a downward one, which may be described as the dilation and contraction of the cultural life of society. When the pendulum swings low and truth and righteousness are low, the necessity arises for the birth of an *Avatara*. The *Gita* says : " Whenever there is decline of *Dharma* (truth and righteousness) and rise of *Adharma* (its opposite), then I body Myself forth. For the protection of the good, for the destruction of the wicked, and for the establishment of *Dharma,* I come into being in every age " (IV, 7, 8).

The object and necessity of a Divine incarnation are therefore to establish the eternal truth, the eternal spirit of religion, by his own living example, God descends upon earth in the form of a man to instruct man how to ascend towards Godhead. Thus does the *Avatara* really become the way, the truth and the light.

Swami Saradananda, one of the foremost disciples of Sri Ramakrishna, has beautifully summarized the characteristics of an *Avatara* : " The first and foremost of these is that they (the *Avataras*) are born free. In the endless struggle and hardship which they undergo to discover the path to super-consciousness, they are prompted always by their desire to enrich the lives of their fellow beings, and not by any selfish motive whatsoever. Indeed, every action in their lives proceeds from such a motive.

" Secondly, they are born endowed with perfect memory. This enables them to remember their former births and the deeds which they accomplished in those. It helps them besides to remember always the utterly transitory nature of human life and its enjoyments, and makes them run to the goal as fast as possible. And by means of this power they are able moreover to compare the present with the past and find out the direction along which the development of people's mind has proceeded hitherto, and the means which would help them to grow and reach the goal quickly in the future. Thirdly, they are discoverers of new paths in the field of

religion. Fourthly, they are able to transmit knowledge to their fellow beings simply by touching them
or even by their will-power. Fifthly, they are able
to perceive clearly, at the very first sight, the *Sams-
karas* or tendencies produced by past *Karmas* of
their fellow beings, although they are never eager to
make a show of that power to others : and that helps
them to know instantly what would help each one
of them to reach easily the highest stage of super-
consciousness. Thus they are the born spiritual
guides of humanity. And, lastly, they are conscious
of their mission throughout their lives."

VI

We have already seen that the purpose of life
Ethics and Moral should be to break down the
Disciplines. barrier of the ego and realise
Brahman, the innermost Self in
all beings, and that the means to that end is to see
the one Self revealed in all and to love all equally.
So the man of attainment, who has arrived at the
goal of Divine consciousness or *Brahma-nirvana,*
devotes his life to the service of all ; and one who
aspires to the Divine state should likewise devote
himself to the service of God in humanity. "He
who judges of pleasure or pain everywhere, by the
same standard as he applies to himself, that *Yogi* is
regarded as the highest" (VI, 32). And we find
this truth echoed in a different setting, and amongst

a different race, when Jesus of Nazareth declared :
" Therefore all things whatsoever ye would that
men should do unto you, do ye even so unto them : for
this is the law and the prophets " (*St. Matt.*
7, 12).

The inner life of man must possess perfect tranquillity, and freedom from passions and passionate
desires, in order that he may realize the blissful
Brahman. This tranquillity is not, in the words of
Aurobindo, " an indolence, incapacity, insensibility,
inertia ; it is full of immortal power, capable of all
action, attuned to deepest delight, open to profoundest love and compassion and to every manner
of intensest *Ananda* (bliss)."

To gain this tranquillity, there is involved the
practice of self-control. Samkara sums up the whole
in one pregnant sentence : " By whom is the world
conquered ? By him who has conquered his own
mind." By self-control is not meant the repressions
and inhibitions so much talked about in the language
of the recent psychology of the West, for this very
thing is condemned by Sri Krishna in unmistakable
terms : " He who, restraining the organs of action,
sits revolving in the mind, thoughts regarding objects
of the senses, he, of deluded understanding, is called
a hypocrite " (III, 6). But the behaviouristic remedy
of giving free play to all impulses and all desires,
which is creating a condition of moral chaos among
the youths of to-day, is not the remedy offered
by the *Gita.* " The turbulent senses do violently

snatch away the mind of even a wise man, striving after perfection. The steadfast, having controlled them all, sits with his mind focussed on Me as the Supreme. His wisdom is steady, whose senses are under control "[1] (II, 60, 61).

This ideal of control means in short the directing of the thoughts and energies of the mind towards a higher ideal. Direction rather than repression, is the method of the Hindus for control of the operations of the mind. " No knowledge of the Self has the unsteady. Nor has he meditation. To the un-meditative there is no peace. And how can one without peace have happiness ? For the mind which follows in the wake of the wandering senses carries away his discrimination, as a wind carries away from its course a boat on the waters " (II, 66, 67).

A further distinction is made in the *Gita* between the divine man and the *Asura* or demoniac man. The one moves towards the attainment of liberation as the other moves away from God to plunge down to lower births and deeper sufferings.

" Fearlessness, purity of heart, steadfastness in knowledge and *Yoga*, giving of charity, control of the senses, *Yajna* (sacrifice), reading of the scriptures, austerity, uprightness ; non-injuriousness, truth, absence of anger, renunciation, tranquillity,

---

[1] *Cf.* Christ's words : " Be ye therefore perfect even as your Father which is in Heaven is perfect." (*Matt.* 5, 48). In fact the entire *Imitation of Christ* may be defined as a striving after perfection and mastery of self.

absence of calumny, compassion, non-covetousness, gentleness, modesty, absence of fickleness, boldness, forgiveness, fortitude, purity, absence of hatred, absence of pride ;—these belong to one born to a divine state. Ostentation, arrogance, self-conceit, anger, as also harshness and ignorance, belong to one who is born to an *Asura* state " (XVI, 1-4).

Describing evil qualities further, the teacher concludes : " Triple is this gate of hell, destructive of the Self—lust, anger and greed ; therefore one should forsake these three " (XVI, 21).

One more point is to be considered regarding self-control and the moral life. The *Gita* lays great stress on self-exertion for the sake of self-improvement, and at the same time exalts Divine grace and the need for us to surrender ourselves to God. " The self is to be saved by one's own self " ; so must one ' exert oneself '. Buddha laid stress on self-exertion and Christ on Divine grace. But these two stand reconciled in the life of a man who has become absorbed in a godly life. He is aware that he must strive, and through his strivings he ultimately learns that all the success he gains is only by Divine grace. This is what is meant by reliance upon a higher will. Sri Ramakrishna expressed this truth in these words : " The breeze of Divine grace is blowing upon all. But one needs to set the sail to feel this breeze of grace."

11

VII

The *Gita* is considered a handbook of practical living as well as a guide to spiritual attainment. In fact, practical life, if rightly pursued, follows one of the paths towards the spiritual life. These paths are known as *Yogas,* which we have briefly discussed in a previous section of this book.

The Yogas :
1. General Considerations.

The word *Yoga* literally means yoking or union (the two words *Yoga* and yoke are derived from the same root), just as the word religion (*re,* again, and *ligo,* to bind) has a similar derivation. The distinctions between individuals—their finiteness and limitedness—are caused, as we have noted again and again, by ignorance, and do not represent the true nature of man. Until the barrier of ego is broken down and the union with the true Self is consummated, one cannot attain the Kingdom of God within. The word *Yoga* defines the methods by which that union with God in man is made possible. Many are the paths by which one may travel to attain this one destination. " So many religions, so many paths." Hindu philosophy recognizes four main paths (*Yogas*) to attainment. They are, as elsewhere indicated, *Jnana Yoga,* the path of knowledge ; *Karma Yoga,* the path of action ; *Bhakti Yoga,* the path of devotion or love ; and *Raja Yoga,* the path of meditation.

Each of these *Yogas* is an independent path to God, and when the end is attained, all four seem to blend in one. Supreme love, divine knowledge, true meditation, and true and divine action are at last identical and cannot be differentiated from one another. The *Gita* insists that they must be both followed and blended not only when the end is reached but as paths to travel. Man is a complex of faculties—reason, will, emotion and the impulse to action—and he must seek union with God through all of them. He must be active as well as meditative ; he must cultivate his intelligence and seek the supreme knowledge as well as cultivate love for the Divine Being ;—such in short is the *Yoga* ideal as taught in the *Gita.*

2. Jnana Yoga.   *Jnana Yoga* literally means the path of union through knowledge. It has come to connote the path of intellectual analysis leading to the immediate perception (*Anubhuti*) of God, who is both transcendent and immanent, who is the inner reality of both man and the universe. Philosophic reasoning does not imply merely intellectual ratiocination, but something more, for man's unaided intellect cannot lead him to God. There must be in addition a transformation of life and conduct, a conversion of the soul, before the knowledge of God or the Self can be attained. Thus says the *Gita* : " Some look upon the Self as marvellous. Others speak of It as wonderful. Others again hear of It as a wonder. And still others,

though hearing, do not understand It at all "
(II, 29).

In order to attain this immediate realization and
understanding of the Self, *Jnana Yoga* advocates
certain disciplines to be practised after the process
of ratiocination.

First of all, the philosopher must learn to dis-
criminate between the real and the unreal. The
opening chapters of the *Gita* explain this process
of discrimination : " The unreal never is. The Real
never is not. Men possessed of the knowledge of
Truth fully know both of these " (II, 16).

The only abiding reality—the immutable, the
illimitable, the indestructible reality—is that by
which the whole universe is pervaded. That is the
same as the Self in man and the reality in the
universe. Whatever we perceive or sense or experience has both beginning and end ; therefore
must our faculty of discrimination lead us to hold
fast to the abiding reality, the Self or God, in the
midst of the fleeting objects and the experiences of
life and of death. " That calm man who is the same
in pain and pleasure, whom these cannot disturb,
alone is able to attain to immortality " (II, 15).

Since we know this Self alone to be real, we should
renounce desire for pleasure and learn to realise the
great source of happiness in the Self within. " When
a man completely casts away all the desires of the
mind, satisfied in the Self alone by the Self, then is
he said to be one of steady wisdom " (II, 55).

To follow the path of philosophy is also to follow the path of self-control, and the *Gita* emphasises this truth in a passage already quoted, in which the unmeditative is compared to a boat carried by the wind out of its course (II, 66-67).

Jnana Yoga is the very process of ' *Neti, Neti* ', ' not this, not this ', which we considered in our study of the *Upanishads*. That is, the Self must not be identified with impermanent entities like the body, the mind and the senses, or with any object and instrument of experience. When a person has become an adept in detaching his true Self from non-self, he becomes blessed with the vision of the Divine, and there dawns upon him the knowledge of the Self in all and all in the Self.

Following the path of knowledge and discrimination does not, however, imply inactivity or giving up the normal activities of life. What one is required to do is to regard the body as the house in which one abides, and the mind and the senses as the instruments of living, to all of which the Lord is the witness. Such a person acts but does not identify himself with his actions. He experiences the objective universe but he has learned to detach himself from his experiences.

Activity, we have already noted, is not opposed to the highest wisdom. An individual who has attained the highest knowledge and supreme peace, though he has nothing to gain by his actions, nor anything to

3. Karma Yoga.

lose by inactivity, yet works, not however for himself as the doer, but, through exercise of his mind, senses and body, as instruments of his true Self, which he has identified with the true Lord of the universe. Never forgetful of his true Self, he is for ever united in the consciousness of God ; knowing that the one Self exists in all, he engages himself in the service of God in all. Intense rest in the midst of intense activity is the experience of such a man of steady wisdom. " He who sees inaction in action, and action in inaction, he is intelligent among men, he is a *Yogi* and a doer of all action " (IV, 18).

Thus a perfected soul, though active in the world of impermanence, unites his consciousness with God, and, says the *Gita,* a man desiring perfection may have this union with God through these very activities in the outer world. This is just what is meant by *Karma Yoga.* Before the advent of Sri Krishna there came a period in the spiritual life of India when the teachings of the *Upanishads* were misunderstood and misinterpreted. We have seen that, according to the scriptures, knowledge alone can give freedom or salvation, but knowledge cannot be acquired through action. The law of *Karma* moreover, teaches how *Karma* creates bondage. And over and above all these concerns of life in the world is the ideal of renunciation of worldly things. The *Upanishads* are actually saturated with this doctrine of renunciation. In course of time these teachings, when not thoroughly understood, led inevitably to the belief in passivism as the supreme state of attainment. The opening chapters of the *Gita* tell how the disciple Arjuna, confused as to the right path and the right conduct to choose, turned to Krishna for counsel. Krishna, the god incarnate, then gave the true interpretation of the teachings of the *Upanishads*. Renunciation, he pointed out, is not renunciation of the world but of worldliness, not of actions but of desires. *Karma* leads to bondage if it increases the weight of desires and magnifies the ego ; it leads to freedom if it helps to deny the self or to free one from attachment to the fruits of actions. Sri Rama-krishna, in modern age, has illustrated this interpretation of *Karma Yoga* and the ideal of renunciation by his famous simile of a boat staying on water.

" Let the boat stay on water," he said, " but let not the water stay in the boat. So let a man live in the world, but let not the world live in him." That is, be in the world but be not of it.

Work, but be not attached to the fruits of actions. " To work you have the right, but not to the fruits thereof."

The *Upanishads* teach that knowledge alone can give freedom, and that infinite knowledge is stored in the soul of man. The very nature of the Self implies not only immortality and perfect bliss but also *Chit* or Pure Consciousness. " The infinite knowledge, which is the Self, is covered by the

shadows of ignorance—hence man's delusion." The
Gita clarifies the issue by teaching the secret of
work, namely, that we must so work that every act
will help to unfold the knowledge of the Self by
removing the ignorance of the ego. The one aim and
the true goal of *Karma Yoga* is the union of one's
self with God through action. Not through any
special actions do we accomplish this, but through
our *Svadharmas*—the particular duties suited to our
natures and the law of our beings, performed as a
means to that end. "Whatever you do, do as
worship unto God."

In order to learn this union with God through
activity, we must also possess
tranquillity and the peace that
comes through meditation. Since to the unmeditative man no peace will come, the *Gita* puts emphasis
upon the practice of meditation, technically known
as *Raja Yoga.* Pantanjali explains *Raja Yoga*
as an eightfold path consisting of *Yama* (moral
disciplines), *Niyama* (religious disciplines), *Asana*
(posture), *Pranayama* (breathing exercises), *Pratya-
hara* (gathering the mind from the thraldom of
the senses), *Dharana* (concentration), *Dhyana*
(meditation) and *Samadhi* (superconscious state).
The *Gita* does not systematically explain these
eight steps, yet they are implied in its teachings
on meditation. The main stress is laid on stilling
the restless mind and becoming absorbed in the
consciousness of the divine Self.

4. Raja Yoga.

" Through whatever reason the restless, unsteady mind wanders away, let him, curbing it from that, bring it under the subjugation of the Self alone. Verily, supreme bliss comes to that Yogi of perfectly tranquil mind whose passions are quieted, who is pure and who has become one with *Brahman* (X, 26, 27). As a lamp in a spot sheltered from the wind does not flicker, even such has been the simile used for a *Yogi* of subdued mind, practising concentration of the Self. When the mind, absolutely restrained by the practice of concentration, attains quietude, and when seeing the Self by the self, one is satisfied in his own Self ; when he feels that infinite bliss— which is perceived by the (purified) intellect and which transcends the senses, and established where-in he never departs from his real state ; and having obtained which, he regards no other acquisition superior to that, and where established, he is not moved even by heavy sorrow—let that be known as the state, called by the name of *Yoga,* a state of severance from the contact of pain. This *Yoga* should be practised with per-severance, undisturbed by depression of heart " (VI, 19-23).

In connection with this practice of *Yoga,* the *Gita* counsels moderation in eating, drinking, sleeping and recreation. Extremes must be avoided, and in unmistakable terms Sri Krishna condemns extreme practice of austerities in the name of *Yoga.*

Knowledge is not of the dry intellectual kind;
neither is meditation directed to
some dry or abstract principle;
rather, they are knowledge of, and meditation upon,
Him who is *Rasa* or full of bliss, and is love itself.
The pursuit of a spiritual ideal is ever accomplished
in an atmosphere of joy where no sorrows enter.
Sorrow itself, which for an aspirant can be only the
sorrow of separation from the Beloved Lord, is also
tinged with joy; for there is always present the
expectancy of union with the source of joy and love.
In separation as in union with God, the aspirant as
well as the perfected soul live in continuous adoration of the Infinite. *Bhakti Yoga* or the path of
love is this adoration and worship in continuous
worship of the Lord, who is the inner Being, the
Self in man, and the embodiment of love and all
blessed qualities. The teachings of the *Gita* em-
phasise a 'whole-souled devotion' to the Supreme,
as the devotee is required constantly to recall the
presence of the all-pervading, all-blissful God.
"Even if the very wicked worships Me, with
devotion to none else, he should be regarded as
good, for he has rightly resolved. Soon does he
become righteous; and attains to eternal peace.
Boldly canst thou proclaim that My devotee is
never destroyed" (IX, 30, 31).

The culmination of *Bhakti Yoga,* and in fact of
all *Yogas,* is the complete, unconditional surrender
of the lower self or ego to God or the Supreme Self.

5. Bhakti Yoga.

When the barrier of ego is removed, either by following the path of knowledge, or of work, or of love, or of meditation, by any or all of these means, the omnipresent, omniscient, immortal Lord of the universe becomes revealed as the Lord of the heart —the Supreme Self.